Mindful Romance

FIGHT LESS...LOVE MORE

*A Breakthrough Guide for
a Lasting Relationship*

DR. TONY O'DONNELL, Ph.D.

EMERALD ISLE
MEDIA

Emerald Isle Media
© 2014 Dr. Tony O'Donnell, Ph.D.

ISBN 978-0-9863576-0-2 (pbk.)
ISBN 978-0-9863576-1-9 (e-book)

First Edition, First Printing, December 2014
Printed in the United States of America

Cover Design by Patricia Bacall, Bacall:Creative
Composition by Anne M. Landgraf, Brooklyn BookWorks

To My Mom and Dad,
married 50 years—rest peacefully
with the Angels in heaven.

Contents

ACKNOWLEDGEMENTS

Many thanks as always to my team that helped shape this manuscript.

Patricia Bacall—your book cover designs are simply magnificent; Anne Landgraf, thank you—your work is flawless; Huck Parks, your work is priceless.

To Dr. John Gray—thanks for inspiring me—my relationships are better because of you.

To my family, both here in America and in Ireland—you are deeply loved.

To my fellow broadcasters, publicists, tv producers, and network stations nationwide—thanks for allowing me to be your guest continually, especially my friends at channel 3 CNN Arizona—with much love and deep appreciation.

To all couples—may your relationships be enhanced by reading this book—and may you find bliss in every breath.

To my parents who had a wonderful marriage for 50 years; you are both loved and deeply missed. I love you so much.

To God who inspires me daily—you have been my strength, my light, my rock, and my comfort during my most challenging times.

Blessings,
Dr. Tony O'Donnell, Ph.D.

INTRODUCTION

Nowadays, things just aren't the way they used to be. That's true of a lot of things of course, and it's especially true of relationships between men and women, particularly where marriage is concerned. The evolution of men and women has changed significantly because many women now are the providers in the home. The whole dichotomy of relationships has changed dramatically from the old days of forty to fifty years ago when the man worked and the woman stayed at home, when she was the caretaker and the man worked outside of the house.

Excessive spending pressures brought on by the rising cost of living have hugely altered the situation. Wages are not rising as fast as inflation. The cost of food, housing, transportation, entertainment, and other major expenses such as putting kids through school have made it more difficult to make ends meet. Couples both commonly work outside the home and this can cause relationships to be stressed to the max. There's financial stress, emotional stress, physical stress, and the stress of jobs. We're tied up in knots with obligations of work, meetings, errands, chores, and kids' activities. There's no connection, there's no love-making, there's little or no joy in the relationship.

I'll call upon the wisdom of other experts in the field for further insights into how you can make your relationships the best they can be. This will include people like John Gray, successful author of the *Men are from Mars, Women are From Venus* books. His message basically is that women are really sensitive by nature while men, although capable of being sensitive, are not that way naturally because of their hunter-gatherer biological makeup. Ancient men had to be strong to protect their families; if they were sensitive, they'd get eaten by a lion! So modern men are descended from men who had to be strong, who had to know what to do to fight back, and that's what comes naturally to them. Being aware of these differences, understanding them, and making allowances for them is one of the keys to a healthy relationship.

It is my hope that this volume will help you have a better marriage, a stronger relationship, be more in love, fight less, communicate effectively, listen without talking, in short, be more mindful of each other instead of mindless. Together, we'll look into the things you can do to carve out the time you need to generate more fun and more passion in your relationship.

I recently spoke at a relationships conference in Las Vegas and during my presentation, I pulled a lot of people out of the audience to get their experiences and perspectives. It went over very well, they really loved hearing about all the factors that go into relationships, how they can go wrong, and what we can do to make them right again. I talked about the role of hormones and how we need to balance them in order for us to effect change and feel better and more aware. I spoke mainly about gender differences, why there's so much conflict, why we need to fight less, how to have true connection, how to get to first base if you wish, what holds us back from true love, listening more, being still and really hearing what the other person is saying. And these are all things I will deal with in depth in this book.

It all comes down to one thing, which at the end of the day is communication. That is the major cause of breakups: we don't listen to each other because we're too busy. We don't take the time. It's important that couples spend quiet times alone, away from the house, away from the children so that they can regroup, so that they can really connect and start to have a better quality of life. Because if couples continue on this vicious cycle of working, working, working and not spending quality time connecting, then they are in real danger of winding up going their separate ways, particularly if the stress levels are exceedingly high.

In my first chapter I'll take a close look at the divorce statistics, and they're not encouraging. For instance, some recent figures put the rate of divorce at nearly five per one thousand people. Substance abuse issues in the home—primarily with alcohol—is one of the big reasons for this phenomenon. Women drink just as much as men. Women are having more affairs now, according to research, than men. So the gender role has shifted significantly because there's no connection, and when there's no connection, then partners go seek out other relationships, whether it's heterosexual or even gay, lesbian, whatever. It becomes a huge issue.

So we'll see at the beginning of the first chapter just what a serious and indeed worrisome a situation this is, but throughout most of this book we'll also see that there's plenty of hope for successful relationships—be it maintaining a good one, finding a new one, or fixing a broken one.

There are many things you can do to promote a healthy relationship, and we'll examine them in the chapters that follow, but perhaps the most basic thing you can do is to simply not give up— to keep working through your differences. My mother and father, God rest them, were married for fifty years and though they sometimes had tough times together, they didn't walk away. A man I met in Vegas one time proudly told me that he had been married for forty-four years before his wife died. He just said it was all about giving her the money and letting her do what she needed to do with the household items. That was the old fashioned way, that doesn't happen nowadays. He said it was all about honor and respect, and that they never fought over anything. She knew he was the man, though.

Women want men to be men and men want women to be women. We wish to give them their independence. We don't want to fight with them. Women think we want to fight with them but we don't at all. It's what we say to each other that causes the fights.

In the following pages we will learn simple remedies to minimize conflict. We'll see the value of communication in reducing conflict and how things like just being a good listener and paying attention to your partner can help us improve it. We'll examine the profound differences in what women want and what men want out of a relationship, cultural and gender differences, and how to save a relationship when one of the partners strays. We'll learn how to stop complaining, how to feel understood, when to apologize (hint: the quicker the better), and when to walk away and take a time out. The presence of children plays a huge role in the dynamics of relationships, so we'll look at important things you can do to make that a positive factor, from implementing regular chores and discipline routines to planning stress-relieving family nights and vacations.

This fast-paced modern life, including the crazy world of social media like Facebook, Twitter, etc., can seem overwhelming and it can feel like we're being stressed to the hilt. Happily, there are some simple, basic things we can do to take control of our lives, slow the pace, sort out the chaos, unwind, relax, and connect. Let's get started!

CHAPTER 1

DIVORCE:
THE ULTIMATE BREAKUP

We begin this examination of relationships with a look at that most dramatic manifestation of a shattered relationship—divorce. Marriage is universally regarded as an exalted institution, one that has been idealized in society and held up in literature as "a metaphor for order and harmony restored, for the broken, disrupted world mended and made right," as the writer Francine Prose put it in a *New York Times Book Review* essay. "We understand that periods of misery and horror alternate with eras of relative tranquility and peace. We want to believe in enduring love partly because we know that we will always be subject to, and at the mercy of, the pendulum swing between chaos and cohesion, happiness and heartbreak."

Everyone agrees that divorce is something that should be avoided not only because of the emotional trauma it causes—especially if children are present—but because of the great amount of expense and time it involves. Yet divorce has become commonplace in the United States, which has the highest rate of divorce in the world. It's been estimated that approximately 45 percent of marriages end in divorce. It's quite remarkable that we're spending millions of dollars, as hard as that is to believe, on legal costs, court costs, child custody battles, separation of homes, relationships with other family members, alienation of the children. When couples break up oftentimes it's because the individuals don't respect each other or don't listen to each other—it's a huge issue. Divorce is the ultimate breakup.

"The dissolution of a marriage is a legal act that may not always coincide with a couple's emotional tearing asunder," states an article on the issue on *Psychology Today*'s website. "Divorce is typically a painful process for all concerned. While it can take adults time to regain psychological equilibrium, whether or not children ever recover a stable perspective continues to be debated. Post-divorce hostility between adults, in addition to directly harming kids, is a sure indicator that the emotional split is incomplete," it adds.

Divorce has become more and more common since the 1900s with a marked increase in the 1970s linked to the initiation of no-fault divorce, *Psychology Today* notes. "Some experts contend that the easing of divorce laws has helped make marriage stronger by rooting it more deeply in personal choice, although it does little to give people the skills needed to work out the inevitable difficulties that arise in a marriage."

It seems that through the passage of time, divorce has become less socially unacceptable while marriage has become less sacred. Young people in general seem to have a far more casual attitude toward the institution than their forebears, reflecting changes in modern values and attitudes. Young love may be beautiful, but it doesn't translate into a successful marriage, as couples who get married before their eighteenth birthdays are the most likely to divorce, according to the website Laws.com, which notes that about 10 percent of the U.S. population is divorced.

Those marriages at the other end of the age spectrum seem to be becoming more vulnerable too, according to a February 2014 story on National Public Radio's "All Things Considered." Citing research which indicates that Americans over the age of fifty are now twice as likely to divorce as people in the age group were 20 years ago, reporter Ina Jaffe commented, "For baby boomers, divorce has become, like marriage, another rite of passage." In the story, researcher Susan Brown, a sociologist with Bowling Green State University, said, "Back in 1990, fewer than one in ten persons who got divorced was over the age of fifty. But today, one in four people getting divorced is fifty or older."

Brown pointed to the "increasing economic independence of women" as one possible explanation for the rise. "Many no longer have to choose between a bad marriage and poverty." The fact that people are living longer now also plays a role in the phenomenon. "When you retire and you no longer have any children at home and you're spending 24/7 with your spouse," Brown surmised, "if this is someone that you're not too fond of anymore, you might want to get divorced because you realize, 'hey, I could spend another twenty, twenty-five years with this person.' "

The website Ask.com lists the rate of divorce for first marriages at from 40 percent to 50 percent, while Census.gov statistics indicate that first marriages last eight years on average. Second marriages are even more fragile, the Ask.com figures show, as 60 percent to 67 percent end in divorce. And if you're hoping the third time is the charm for your marriage, the statistics aren't encouraging: third go-rounds strike out nearly three-quarters of the time.

In his incisive and useful book, *The Seven Principles for Making Marriage Work*, John M. Gottman, PhD, comments on the "dire" statistics concerning divorce. The chance of a first marriage ending in divorce over a forty-year period is 67 percent," he says. "Half of all divorces will occur in the first seven years. Some studies find the divorce rate for second marriages is as much as 10 percent higher than for first-timers. The chance of getting divorced remains so high that it makes sense for all married couples—including those who are currently satisfied with their relationship—to put extra effort into their marriages to keep them strong."

Most often, it's the woman who initiates divorce proceedings, figures show. This is especially true among married couples with children, as women seek legal separation in those situations two-thirds of the time. States with the highest instances of divorce include Nevada, Arkansas, Oklahoma, and West Virginia, all of which have divorce rates in excess of five per 1,000 people. Divorce is least common in the District of Columbia, Illinois, Iowa, Maryland, Massachusetts, New Jersey, New York, North Dakota, Pennsylvania, and Wisconsin, where the rate hovers just below three per 1,000 people.

The reasons couples divorce are as varied as the individuals involved and are often driven by the factors unique to their personalities, of course, but a range of studies have revealed some interesting common contributing factors. For instance, a Swedish survey published in the *British Journal of Urban Studies* found a connection between couples who had long commutes to work and the likelihood that their unions would end in dissolution. The divorce rate for all couples in the ten-year study was 11 percent, but for those in which at least one of the partners had to drive forty-five miles or more to work (one way) the rate was as much as 14 percent. The research indicated, though, that if the marriages were able to survive the strain of such lengthy daily separations for five years or more, divorce became less likely.

Another intriguing factor was revealed in a University of Michigan study, in which participants were found to be 20 percent less likely to divorce in marriages where the man thought of himself as having a "close" relationship with his wife's family. Interestingly, the likelihood of divorce was actually 20 percent higher, the research indicated, in marriages in which the woman said she had a close relationship with her husband's family.

The number of children in a marriage was seen as a positive factor—within limits—in another study conducted at Ohio State University. The research, which was based on interviews with 57,000 adults over a thirty-year period ending in 2012, showed that the subjects' divorce rate dropped by around 2 percent per child, up to seven children.

Along with the sizable financial cost, the emotional toll divorce takes on those affected by it—from the couple themselves, to their children, their immediate families, their friends, and their co-workers—is outwardly apparent and understood. Perhaps less obvious is the adverse effect divorce has on its participants' health. Young people with less fully developed coping skills can be particularly impacted, a Michigan State University study found.

Dr. Gottman cites another study, conducted by Lois Verbrugge and James House of the University of Michigan, which suggested that "an unhappy marriage can increase your chances of getting sick by roughly 35 percent and even shorten your life by an average of four years." On the other hand, Dr. Gottman notes, "People who are happily married live longer, healthier lives than either divorced people or those who are unhappily married. Scientists know for certain that these differences exist, but we are not yet sure why," he says.

"Part of the answer," Dr. Gottman points out, "may simply be that in an unhappy marriage, people experience chronic, diffuse physiological arousal—in other words, they feel physically stressed and usually emotionally stressed as well. This puts added wear and tear on the body and mind, which can present itself in any number of physical ailments, including high blood pressure and heart disease, and in a host of psychological ones, including anxiety, depression, suicide, violence, psychosis, homicide, and substance abuse."

Dr. Gottman, a professor at the University of Washington, continues: "Not surprisingly, happily married couples have a far lower rate of such maladies. They also tend to be more health-conscious than others. Researchers theorize that this is because spouses keep after each other to have regular checkups, take medicine, eat nutritiously, and so on. Recently, my laboratory uncovered some exciting, preliminary evidence that a good marriage may also keep you healthier by directly benefitting your immune system, which spearheads the body's defenses against illness. Researchers have known for about a decade that divorce can depress the immune system's function. Theoretically this lowering in the system's ability to fight foreign invaders could leave you open to more infectious diseases and cancers. Now we have found that the opposite may also be true. Not only do happily married people avoid this drop in immune function, but their immune systems may even be getting an extra boost."

The assertion of the healthful effects of marriage was given further credence by a Harvard Medical School study whose findings included a tendency for married individuals to have lower blood pressure than their non-married counterparts. The two-year, randomized, controlled study, which was published in early 2014 in *The Journal of Hypertension*, involved 325 adults—roughly half married and half non-married—who were directed to follow specific diets and whose blood pressure was measured around the clock by special devices.

The guiding principle behind the research was the fact that most individuals' blood pressure levels usually follow a daily cycle in which they rise throughout the morning and afternoon before falling again at night, usually by approximately 10 percent. The researchers found that the cycle, which is considered normal and conducive to cardiovascular health and lower mortality, was more common among the study's married subjects than it was among the non-married control group. According to an account in *The New York Times*, the report showed that "people who were married—especially men—were much more likely to exhibit this 'nocturnal dipping' than those who were not married . . . even after taking into account factors like socioeconomic status, age, diet, and body mass index. The researchers speculate that marriage might provide a level of social support that leads people to better manage their health and stress levels. Or, they wrote, 'being married may simply be a marker for those with better overall health status, nutritional status, and psychiatric wellness.' "

Recognizing when a marriage is in trouble, then, is likely to be crucial to your physical as well as your psychic wellbeing. An expert of more than twenty years standing in the field of couples' relationships, Dr. Gottman asserts that the strongest indicator of a marriage on the brink of failure is when the spouses become contemptuous of each other. Prime evidence of this is when disrespectful and demanding language creeps into everyday discourse. Writing on the *Psychology Today* website, professor, presenter, personal coach, and author Preston Ni breaks this down into four primary styles of communication: "You . . . " declarations, Universal statements, ad hominem arguments focused on the other person rather than the issue, and attempts to invalidate the other person's feelings.

Ni defines "You" declarations as those that include accusations such as, "You are not good enough," "You should pay attention," "You need to do this now," "You have to understand my position," and "You better get it right." He comments: "Most people don't like being judged or told what to do, and when we use 'you' language plus directives, it's easy to arouse in others feelings of resentment and defensiveness. This type of communication is also problematic in that it tends to invite a 'no' response, resulting in disagreements and conflicts," he says.

The next category, universal statements, is characterized by "expressions that generalize a person's character or behavior in a negative way," Ni writes. "The most common types of universal statements involve the use of words such as 'always,' 'never,' 'again,' 'so,' 'every time,' 'such a,' and 'everyone.' Universal statements are often used in combination with 'you' language. For example: 'You always leave the toilet seat up.' 'You never put the tooth paste cap back on.' 'You're messing up again!' 'You are so lazy!' 'You forget to do this every time!' 'You're such a slob!' 'Everyone knows that you're bad.' "

Universal statements are corrosive in a relationship because they show how convinced the speaker is that they are right and their partner is wrong, Ni explains. "There is no possibility of the listener being any other way. The potential to change is discounted." Because such statements "point out 'what is wrong,' instead of 'how to be better,'" he says, they "actually discourage change. Still another destructive aspect of universal statements is that they are very likely to incite arguments. That's because the claims they contain "can easily be disputed," Ni writes. "If I say to you, 'You never wash the dishes,' all you need to do is come up with one exception, 'That's not true, Preston, I washed the dishes once last year,' and you have successfully contradicted my statement. The general nature of universal statements makes them very vulnerable to specific counterexamples."

The third type of disrespectful communication, ad hominem attacks, are those in which the speaker is "tough on the person, soft on the issue," Ni reveals. "In every communication situation involving another person, there are two elements present: the person you are relating to and the issue or behavior you are addressing. Contemptuous communicators "get personal" by being tough on the person, while minimizing or ignoring the issue or the behavior."

It's important to realize that there are good alternatives, he says. For instance, a statement such as "You are so stupid!" is counter productive as compared to the much more effective, "You're a smart person, and what you did this morning was not very smart." Similarly, a comment like, "I noticed that you didn't do the chores this week," would be far less likely to lead to a row as would the claim, "You never do any chores. You're useless!" Another alternative would be to simply say, "I know you have a lot on your mind lately, and I think it would be good for us to have a date night to reconnect," as opposed to, "You're always forgetting about me—do you even have a clue?," he writes.

"Being tough on the person and soft on the issues can easily arouse negative reactions from the listener, who's likely to take what you're saying personally, and as a result, feel angry, resentful, hurt, or resistant," he explains. "Note that tough on the person and soft on the issue also involves the frequent use of 'you' statements and universals."

The fourth category, the deliberate disregard of a partner's feelings, "occurs when we recognize emotions, positive or negative, coming out of a person, and either discount, belittle, minimize, ignore, or negatively judge these feelings," Ni says. A declaration such as "Your concerns are meaningless to me!" would be one example. Others would include "Your complaints are totally unfounded," "You're blowing things way out of proportion," and "Who cares if you're angry? Stop over-reacting!"

By invalidating the feelings of another person, such remarks "are likely to cause instant resentment," Ni writes. "The person whose feelings we just invalidated is likely to feel hurt and angry. In some cases, a person whose feelings have been invalidated might shut down from you emotionally, so that her/his feelings will not be hurt again."

So the presence of such characteristics in a relationship are a sign of likely dissolution. They "work like poison," according to Ni. "They destroy the health and well-being of a close, personal bond." Likely, but not inevitable, and that's why it's important to be aware of those characteristics and look for ways to make a change. It starts with being mindful and not mindless in our interactions with our partners, and that's just what I'll be discussing in the next chapter.

CHAPTER 2

MINDFUL INSTEAD
OF MINDLESS

Communication is so vital to a relationship and one of the main keys to better communication is simply to stop complaining. We saw in the previous chapter how corrosive that can be. Getting it under control is very important, but it's certainly not easy. That's because it really comes naturally to a lot of people. Put plainly, men and women like to complain about each other. It's ironic.

I was a first-hand observer of this phenomenon at a seminar I participated in involving twenty couples. The organizers split us up, the men all going in one room and the women in another, and then had us all talk about the things that drove us crazy and nuts about our partners in a negative way. Then they reunited the group and when we came back and compared notes, we discovered that we were all saying a lot of the same things about each other.

The men were saying, "She doesn't listen," "She makes a big deal out of everything," "She talks too much," "She's very irrational," "She makes a mountain out of a molehill," "She's relentless, she never gives up," "She never forgets and she never fails to remind me of what I've done wrong," "She is very controlling, manipulative, and demanding," "She nags all the time," "She constantly whines and complains," "She withholds sex," "She wants to change me," "She's never satisfied with me," "She's very materialistic," "She only remembers the bad things and overanalyzes," "She gossips too much."

Meanwhile, the women were saying, "He doesn't listen," "He's insensitive," "He tries to 'fix' my emotions," "Instead of listening, he has to control everything," "He seems to be unhappy," "He makes everything about him, he's so self-centered," "He doesn't communicate his emotions," "He takes everything so personally," "He doesn't like to be criticized and is way too sensitive about it," "He thinks he has to be perfect all the time and he can't admit it when he's wrong," "He doesn't share my sense of urgency," "He's so inflexible with his priorities," "He just won't change," "He is oblivious to what's going on around him," "His first response is 'no,'" "It always needs to be his idea," "He blames me for his feelings to save face," "His ego always gets in the way," "Whenever I ask for something he calls me a nag," "He says, 'What do you want me to do?' like he just doesn't get it," "He doesn't notice the dirty clothes on the floor," "He's got too much rage and anger, it's that warrior energy," "He pouts and whines and complains," "He's got a cave mentality," "He's got ADD," "He doesn't spend enough time just getting to know me," "He doesn't appreciate the beauty of femininity," "He doesn't accept me for who I am," "He likes me when I'm up emotionally, but not when I'm down," "He wants sex too soon after a fight," "If I ask him what he thinks, he says, 'whatever you want'—I feel like it's all up to me," "He interrupts me all the time," "If he speaks first and I don't agree, he feels unsupported," "He demands respect," "If he interrupts me when I'm busy and I don't respond immediately, he gets upset but if he's watching sports and I want his attention, I have to wait," "If there's anything wrong with the kids or the house, he thinks it's my fault," "It seems like sex is the answer to everything for him," "If I have some success, he feels intimidated," "He just kicks back and relaxes as soon as he gets in the door," "He avoids discussing big issues," "He doesn't understand foreplay—loving is more than sex and foreplay is not just sexual touching."

So there were a lot of similarities between what the men and women at this seminar were saying about what they felt each other's shortcomings were. It all goes to show that we need to really be more mindful rather than mindless.

We really do need to pay attention to what our partner is saying. And if we do that, we can understand each other better, we can communicate much more effectively, we can really hear and understand what the other person is saying. If we don't, the result usually is a rift. And this is why it's important that we take time outs to really connect and listen and discus issues, particularly as related to finances, the children, and chores in the home, so that we can reduce conflict and keep stress at a minimum and develop more joy and harmony.

For a woman, feeling that she is being listened to and understood is very important. She needs to be understood because, as research has shown, in general, women talk more than men. They have this incessant need to talk, and I say this respectfully and not to be derogatory because women sometimes get really upset when they read an author making claims about how women talk a lot. The simple truth is, many women talk a lot because they have a lot to say.

First of all, this can be an outward manifestation of their maternal instinct, because when women become mothers, they feel compelled to take care of the children. That's their role. In some situations that role is reversed where the mother is working and the husband becomes the stay-at-home mom. That generally is not the case in most situations, but it does happen.

So we all need to be understood. We all need to feel that what we say makes a difference. It's very important for you as a human being to feel that when you speak to another person that he or she hears what you are saying and that what you are communicating does not go over their head. That form of miscommunication happens so much because it's hard for us to be still and it's very hard for us to be mindful and aware of what the other person is saying in every area of our lives. That can happen simply because we're not present. And if we're not present, we can't hear, we can't be understood, and we can't understand what the person is saying and consequently as a result, there's miscommunication, there's a misdirection of the message. And if there's a misdirection of the message, then there's usually a conflict either in that moment or at a later stage in the couple's relationship and that tends to go on and on and on and on if one person doesn't make an effort to listen.

Similarly, there is some research indicating that men are not really great listeners. Well, I don't necessarily believe that that's true of a lot of men, and I don't want to paint all men with a broad brush and say they are bad listeners. Still, men do tend not to listen sometimes, and this can be because they don't always feel that the things that their partner is saying to them are that important. They may regard their partner's comments as just an emotional response to certain feelings. They might dismiss them as the utterances of a woman, perhaps overly stressed, who says more than she really wishes to say, who just needs someone to listen to her. And this is why she calls her girlfriend or girlfriends and they simply talk and talk and talk and talk and talk.

Men don't generally like to hear that kind of stuff. They tend to be more quiet. They tend to be providers. Their job is to provide and protect and to offer security for their partners. They don't really feel it's their job to hear an awful lot of emotional stuff. Emotional stuff tends to be painful for them. It causes them to go into their little cocoon if you will, or go to their room and close the door so that they don't have to deal with it. Or they might go for a walk or go for a hike or go exercising or read a book or watch a movie because it's very difficult for them to comprehend the emotional outbursts that women tend to come up with.

These basic differences in the psyches of men and women can be exaggerated through the workings of an interpersonal dynamic that best-selling author John Gray calls the "See-Saw Effect." In his book, *What You Feel You Can Heal,* Gray says that women who consider themselves to be even tempered can by caught off guard by this effect, in which one partner's suppressed feelings results in the other's outbursts. "I've seen this pattern happen over and over again with women who can't understand why they become so insecure and hysterical around the men they love and men who can't understand why otherwise logical and strong women seem to fall apart around them," he writes. "The answer is the See-Saw Effect. The men are following their conditioning to not show feelings of fear and the women end up expressing all the men's suppressed fearful emotion. The extreme case of this is the controlling, even-tempered husband, never expressing any emotion that could be taken for weakness or self-doubt, driving the wife into overemotionalism and hysteria, then making the woman feel inferior and mentally ill by constantly pointing out how emotional she is becoming. Many women literally end up in mental institutions when this happens to them over a long period of time. And of course, there are cases of the reverse: women controlling themselves and the men exploding with feelings."

This "See-Saw Effect" may also result in a woman becoming ever more "needy" in response to her partner's suppression of his insecurities. Gray gives as an example a man who falls in love with a woman but then becomes increasingly uncomfortable with the need he feels for her. His way of dealing with this need is to suppress it, which creates a tension in the relationship. When the man tries to hide his feelings it causes the woman to overcompensate as she begins to worry that he's starting to withdraw from her. Her out-of-proportion reaction is fueled by her fear of losing him, he explains, "she feels desperate to get a commitment from him; she feels weak in his presence," even though that's not what she's really like at all.

This appearance of increased neediness in her makes her seem hysterical to him and makes her less attractive to him. He doesn't recognize that it's his insecurities that produced it in her.

"This phenomenon is very common in intimate relationships," Gray explains. "What they don't realize is that each woman is reflecting the man's own needs back to him, needs he is afraid to look at and feel."

He cautions, though, that the effect shouldn't be seen as an excuse for dismissing your own anger as merely a reflection of your partner's anger. For example, say a couple goes to a restaurant and starts to become irritated because their dinner is late. The man may try to suppress his anger and also try to calm the woman down. His repression and attempt to quell her anger may actually make her more angry, but it's important to remember that she was already somewhat angry before he started trying to calm her down. As the man continues to hold his feelings down while telling the woman she should do likewise, "the more her feelings will intensify. She was angry also—it's not all (his) anger she is expressing, but now her anger and annoyance in the restaurant will be way out of proportion."

Being aware of the "See-Saw Effect" can be a valuable tool in helping you understand and deal with your emotions. You may have wondered in the past why your partner has reacted so negatively to all your efforts to sooth their feelings, why it only seems to make things worse. "That's because your partner is probably expressing an emotion that you are suppressing," Gray writes. "People close to you will act like mirrors, reflecting back to you a perfect image of yourself, including the parts of yourself you would rather not look at or deal with. So if you are suppressing your fears, your partner may continue to pester you with her fears and worries, as if to hold a mirror up to you and say, 'Hey, take a look at some of the feelings you are pushing down.'"

Therefore, you should understand that "you will resist in your partner what you suppress in yourself," he says. It's only natural that the man, once he has gotten his own emotions under control—or at least suppressed them—will try to do the same with his partner when she starts expressing anger. But because he's holding his own emotions back, Gray reveals, he doesn't recognize that the woman is merely expressing the same feelings. "Trying to change your partner's emotions or talk them out of feeling a feeling is a sure sign that they are mirroring to you an emotion you don't want to feel in yourself," he writes. "If you are resisting your partner's emotions, it's probably because you are resisting those same emotions within yourself."

The "See-Saw Effect" can be difficult to work through, but at least when one of the partners is honestly expressing their emotions, there's some opportunity for talking things out. What's far worse is when both partners fail to allow their emotions to come to the surface, Gray explains. This creates an unsustainable tension, like pressure in a connecting pipe between two tanks both filled with pressurized liquid. Little by little the pressure will build until eventually the pipe bursts. "This is what occurs in many relationships," he declares. "Neither party tells the complete truth about their feelings; they push down their emotions, drift apart, and eventually break their emotional connection entirely. They have successfully repressed all feelings for one another."

Once that connection is broken, it "causes you to feel you have fallen out of love . . . that you have lost your attraction," he relates. "Two people can live comfortably together, if they choose to, once they have broken the connection, because the source of tension will be gone. They will no longer be victims of the See-Saw Effect. But they have lost the love, the passion, and the aliveness in the relationship. And, more importantly, they have lost the opportunity to grow and learn from the mirror of their partner."

You can't change the "See-Saw Effect," Gray points out, because it is a basic characteristic of human relationships. Therefore, being able to recognize it is important because it can help you cope with the difficulties it inevitably produces. When your partner behaves emotionally—whether they are mad, afraid, unhappy, or overly dependent—and you become angry or dissatisfied with them, it's likely because they are "expressing some of what you are suppressing inside. Because you resist your emotions, you will resist your partner's similar emotions. If you are resisting your partner's emotions, it's probably because you are resisting those same emotions within yourself. On the other hand, if your partner expresses a feeling and you don't feel annoyed or irritated and can easily comfort them, you are probably not suppressing any emotions, and they are simply expressing their own feelings," he says.

The effect seems intractable. What could you possibly to do combat it? Well, it turns out there are a few things, according to Gray, that you can do to "prevent yourself and others from unnecessary anguish and hurt." One is to "Start taking responsibility for your emotions—express them instead of suppressing them." Another is "when someone close to you is expressing an emotion and you notice yourself resisting them, stop and ask yourself: 'Are they expressing something I am not willing to experience or look at in myself?'" There are other things that myself, Gray, and others recommend you do, and we'll look at some of these later in the book.

For now, it's important to keep in mind that women should remain less emotional, more present, and more aware, and that men try to be more tolerant so arguments, shouting, fights, conflict, and aggression can be kept at a minimum.

Another way to be mindful of each other is simply by making an effort to connect with each other. As described by Dr. Gottman, the marriage and relationships expert whom we met in the first chapter, it's a matter of turning toward each other rather than away from each other.

"Hollywood has dramatically distorted our notions of romance and what makes passion burn," he writes. "Watching Humphrey Bogart gather teary-eyed Ingrid Bergman into his arms may make your heart pound, but real-life romance is fueled by a far more humdrum approach to staying connected. It is kept alive each time you let your spouse know he or she is valued during the grind of everyday life. Comical as it may sound, romance actually grows when a couple are in the supermarket and the wife says, 'Are we out of bleach?' and the husband says, 'I don't know. Let me go get some just in case,' instead of shrugging apathetically. It grows when you know your spouse is having a bad day at work and you take sixty seconds out of your own workday to leave words of encouragement on his voice mail. It grows when your wife tells you one morning, 'I had the worst nightmare last night,' and you say 'I'm in a big hurry but tell me about it now so we can talk about it tonight,' instead of 'I don't have time.'" Dr. Gottman advises.

"In all of these instances, husband and wife are making a choice to turn toward each other rather than away. In marriage, people periodically make what I call 'bids' for their partner's attention, affection, humor, or support. People either turn toward one another after these bids or they turn away. Turning toward is the basis of emotional connection, romance, passion, and a good sex life," he writes.

It's often the little moments that matter for a couple's healthy relationship, according to Dr. Gottman. Moments like reading a newspaper together or conversing with each other over a meal. "Couples who turn toward each other remain emotionally engaged and stay married. Those that don't eventually lose their way," he says.

To illustrate the point, Dr. Gottman says that, like money you are setting aside for savings, these little moments can be thought of as something that builds up in a sort of "emotional bank account," becoming an increasing source of strength in the relationship as it grows. "Partners who characteristically turn toward each other rather than away are putting money in the bank. They are building up emotional savings that can serve as a cushion when times get rough, when they're faced with major life stress or conflict. Because they have stored up all this goodwill, they are better able to make allowances for each other when a conflict arises. They can maintain a positive sense of each other and their marriage, even during hard times," he declares.

But the stress-relieving cushion is not the most important benefit of this emotional bank account, it's the "long-lasting relationship" that is provided by "turning toward your spouse in the little ways." A dinner date or a big vacation getaway are fun and can have a rejuvenating effect on a relationship, he says, "but the real secret is to turn toward each other in little ways every day. A romantic night out really turns up the heat only when a couple has kept the pilot light burning by staying in touch in the little ways." For a couple that doesn't have that daily connection in the bank, so to speak, and that hasn't been agreeing in much of anything in their relationship, trying to create closeness with a special event "would most likely be a fiasco, filled with accusations, recriminations, or awkward silences."

If you're not sure whether you've accumulated enough moments in your emotional bank account, whether you've been turning toward each other enough, there are twenty questions Dr. Gottman suggests that couples can ask themselves to find out:

Do you "enjoy doing small things together, like folding laundry or watching TV"?

Do you "look forward to spending . . . free time with (your) partner"?

Do you feel that your partner is happy to see you after you've been apart?

Does your partner make you feel like they are interested in your opinions?

Do you "really enjoy" talking things over with your partner?

Do you feel like your partner is one of your "best friends"?

Do you think your partner feels the same way?

Do you "just love talking to each other"?

Does time seem to fly when you do things together?

Do you "always have a lot to say to each other"?

Would you say that you "always have a lot of fun together"?

Do you consider yourselves to be "spiritually very compatible"?

Do you "tend to share the same basic values"?

Do you "like to spend time together in similar ways"?

Do you "really have a lot of common interests"?

Do you "have many of the same dreams and goals"?

Do you "like to do a lot of the same things"?

Do you still enjoy your partner's interests even where they differ from yours?

Do you "tend to have a good time" no matter what you are doing together? and finally,

Do you tell each other when either of you has a bad day?

In Dr. Gottman's estimation, you only need to answer yes to half of these questions for your relationship to be in a good place emotionally. Ten or more yeses means that "you are so often 'there' for each other during the minor events in your lives, you have built up a hefty emotional bank account that will support you over any rough patches in your marriage (and keep many at bay). It's those little moments that you rarely think about—when you're shopping at the supermarket, folding laundry, or having a quickie catch-up call while you're both still at work—that make up the heart and soul of marriage," he says. "Having a surplus in your emotional bank account is what makes romance last and gets you through hard times, bad moods, and major life changes."

On the other hand, if you honestly had to say no to eleven or more questions, it's time to re-focus your priorities and pay serious attention to rejuvenating your relationship. You need to re-discover the small things that you shared which first endeared you to each other and in so doing "you will make your marriage not only more stable but more romantic," Dr. Gottman writes. "Every time you make the effort to listen and respond to what your spouse says, to help him or her, you make your marriage a little better."

It's the mindfulness rather than mindlessness that I talked about earlier that can be so important to a relationship. So often, it's not outright nastiness that causes insurmountable rifts between two people. Tragically, it can be simple carelessness that leads to misunderstandings that can snowball out of control. Don't let that happen! Share the "boring" moments and live the romance that can be your relationship.

Like Dr. Gottman says, "for many couples, just realizing that they shouldn't take their everyday interactions for granted makes an enormous difference in their relationship. Remind yourself that being helpful to each other will do far more for the strength and passion of your marriage than a two-week Bahamas getaway."

A simple question like "How was your day, dear?", sincerely offered, can sometimes have all the impact of "I love you," especially if your partner has been experiencing a stressful day. In fact, outside stress can adversely affect a relationship. "Couples who are overrun by this stress see their marriages relapse," notes Dr. Gottman, "while those who can help each other cope with it keep their marriages strong."

So if you're present for your partner and engaged in what they're saying about the difficulties they experienced during their day, it can drop the stress levels significantly. But if you are not paying attention, if you're off in your own world and not focusing on what your partner is saying, it not only doesn't help your relationship, it makes things much worse. Frustration will build as your partner realizes that you haven't been treating his or her problems seriously.

"If that's the case," Dr. Gottman asserts, "you need to change your approach to these catch-up conversations to make sure they help you calm down. For starters, think about the timing of the chat. Some people want to unburden themselves when they're barely through the door. But others need to decompress on their own for a while before they're ready to act. So wait until you both want to talk," he advises.

He recommends that you set aside about a half hour a day for these talks. "The cardinal rule is that you talk about whatever is on your mind outside of your marriage. This is not the time to discuss any conflicts between you. It's an opportunity to support each other emotionally concerning other areas in your lives." Couples should employ "active listening" in these sessions, he says, which makes it quite different than the normally recommended procedure for talking through relationship problems. "The goal of active listening is to hear your spouse's perspective with empathy and without judging him or her. That's all well and good. But this approach usually fails because couples are asked to use it when they are airing their gripes with each other. This is difficult to do and often about as painless as an IRS audit. It's virtually impossible not to feel frightened, hurt, or mad as hell when your spouse is blasting you."

But when the talk is about non-threatening matters that don't involve you or your partner personally, the "same listening technique can be extremely beneficial," Dr. Gottman says he has found. "In this context, you'll feel far freer to be readily supportive and understanding of your spouse and vice versa. This can only heighten the love and trust you feel."

It's so important for you two to feel like you're on the same side on something. In fact, "that's one of the foundations of a long-lasting relationship," according to Dr. Gottman. This is true whether you are celebrating some accomplishment or offering "a ready shoulder to cry on." Say your partner is describing a confrontation they had with someone. It could be that you think they might not have been in the right. It doesn't matter. You need to give your partner the benefit of the doubt because it's crucial that they feel that you've got their back.

"Don't side with the opposition—this will make your spouse resentful and dejected," he counsels. "If your wife's boss chewed her out for being five minutes late, don't say, 'Oh well, maybe Bob was just having a bad day.' And certainly don't say, 'Well, you shouldn't have been late.' Instead, say, 'That's so unfair!' The point isn't to be dishonest. It's just that timing is everything. When your partner comes to you for emotional support (rather than for advice), your job is not to cast moral judgment or to tell him or her what to do. Your job is to say, 'poor baby.'" By so doing, you will "let him or her know that the two of you are in this together."

It could be, however, that more basic differences lay at the base of your problems. "For example, when one partner rebuffs the other, it could be a sign of hostility over some festering conflict. But I have found that when one spouse regularly feels the other just doesn't connect enough, often the cause is a disparity between their respective needs for intimacy and independence.

"Marriage is something of a dance," he continues. There are times when you feel drawn to your loved one and times when you feel the need to pull back and replenish your sense of autonomy. There's a wide spectrum of 'normal' needs in this area—some people have a greater and more frequent need for connection, others, for independence. A marriage can work even if people fall opposite ends of this spectrum—as long as they are able to understand the reason for their feelings and respect their differences. If they don't, however, hurt feelings are likely to develop," Dr. Gottman says.

Regardless of where your marriage falls in this spectrum, he advises, you can't let your frustrations remain unspoken. Maybe your partner's reticence in expressing affection makes you feel like you're being ignored. Or maybe your desire for closeness is overwhelming to your partner. Whatever your differences, they have to be brought out into the open and talked over so that you two can bring them to some mutual resolution. "Looking at these moments together will give you greater insight into each other," he relates, "and help you both learn how to give each other what you need."

Above all, he urges, when you are working things out, do it with honor and respect. "When you honor and respect each other, you're usually able to appreciate each other's point of view, even if you don't agree with it. When there's an imbalance of power, there's almost inevitably a great deal of marital distress." Although most commonly, it's the man who tries to exercise the most power in a relationship, "there are wives who have just as hard a time acceding to their spouse's wishes," he notes. Either way, the feeling that one side of the relationship must exert more power than the other must be countered.

It should be clear from what we've seen in this chapter, then, that in any relationship there's going to be conflict. It's inevitable when two distinct individuals with some very fundamental differences have close dealings with each other. What separates a successful relationship from an unsuccessful one, then, is how well the couple handles that conflict. In the next chapter, we'll look at some effective ways of managing those differences and minimizing those conflicts.

CHAPTER 3

COMMUNICATION IS CRUCIAL

Overcoming or compensating for your inherent differences is one of the keys to a strong relationship, and one of the best ways to accomplish that is through open and honest communication. How can you expect your partner to understand and accommodate your true feelings if you are not willing to share them completely? How can you expect to build and strengthen a feeling of trust between you two if you aren't willing to open up to your spouse? And just as it's what you hope for and expect from them, it's what they hope for and expect from you too. Communication is truly a two-way street. If you aren't sensitive to the desires and interests being expressed by your partner, you can't expect your partner to be sensitive to what you are saying. That's just basic common sense, although as we all tend to become caught up in our personal problems and activities from time to time, it's something we all need to be reminded of occasionally.

Effective communication is one where there's plenty of give and take. How do you know if there's enough give and take? Gauge your feelings based on your emotions—are you becoming increasingly frustrated as the conversation goes on? You are probably reacting to a feeling that your partner isn't really listening to what you're saying or you are feeling that your partner isn't taking you seriously enough. Gauge your partner's feelings based on their body language, facial expressions, and tone of voice. Are they becoming increasingly agitated as your conversation goes on? Likely they are getting the impression that what they are saying isn't really getting through to you, that you are just dismissing what they are saying or not hearing it at all.

As for your feelings, let you partner know that you don't think they are giving what you're saying the attention you think it deserves. It's very likely they just aren't aware of it and will appreciate you telling them because they really don't want to hurt you. Keep in mind that in order to be sure your partner isn't getting what you are saying, you have to really listen to their responses. Maybe they really are listening to you and you aren't paying close enough attention to them to realize it. On the other hand, if you perceive agitation in your partner, say so. It will show that you really are listening to them and that you are keyed in to their emotions after all.

And for goodness sake, if there is a miscommunication, don't make a big issue of it. In fact, if you can, by all means find some humor in it and have a good laugh together about it. Say something like: "You thought I wasn't paying attention? I heard every word you were saying (and here repeat some of those words to show you mean it), I just didn't think it was that important—just kidding! Seriously, I'm sorry I looked like I wasn't listening, I was and I really do care about what you have to say."

And if the kidding around gets a little physical at that point, let it happen! It could lead to a moment of intimacy between you and physical closeness can reinforce psychic closeness.

Another great way to connect is to pick topics of conversation that are of interest to both of you. Things like how the kids are doing in school, work that needs to be done around the house, something the neighbor did that amused you both, plans for the weekend, memories of things you've done together in the past. These are all sure-fire ways to establish a feeling of commonality between you and thus bring your relationship closer together.

Definitely there will be times, however, when one or both of you will feel too strongly about your point of view to think it's funny that your partner doesn't agree with you. Not everything can be made light of and some things just have to be hashed out. Take things as far as you can go without outright acrimony and if you hit an absolute impasse, just drop it for a while. A time out, or temporary walk-away, which we'll discuss in more detail later in this book, can really defuse a potentially ugly situation, cooling things down considerably. Try to re-visit the issue later and if you feel you still can't do it without becoming too emotional, I highly recommend bringing the matter to an impartial mediator like a councillor or therapist as a way of arriving at an effective solution. There's nothing like the input of a neutral observer to put your partner's, as well as your own, positions in perspective and maybe enable you see a side to the matter that you hadn't seen before.

But whether it's just between the two of you or in front of a marriage adviser, you need to bring honesty to the table for your communication to be truly effective and your relationship to be thoroughly strong. Indeed, the "essential key," according to John Gray, is that "you must be able to share and express the complete truth about yourself and your feelings."

It's not necessarily the same as "being honest and not lying," he writes in *What You Can Feel, You Can Heal*, "Many times you tell the truth but leave out the important parts. Or, if you don't like the truth, you create a new truth. Do you ever smile when you are really angry?" Dr. Gray asks. "Have you ever acted mean and angry when deep inside you were really afraid? Do you ever laugh and make light of something when you feel very sad and rejected? Have you ever blamed another when you were the one feeling guilty? This is what I mean by not telling the complete truth."

Being able to convey your true feelings "is the first step in resolving emotional tension and enriching your relationships with others. Before you can communicate the truth about what you feel, you have to know what you are feeling in the first place," he explains. "As human beings, we are experts at hiding the truth about what we are feeling. We become masters of disguising what we really feel inside, and therefore we end up hiding and suppressing who we really are. You may become so good at hiding the truth from yourself that you even start to believe your own lies. Gradually you may lose touch with what you really feel, and even if you want to tell the truth about what is going on inside, you can't," he warns.

"Your ability to feel love is directly proportional to your ability to tell the complete truth. The more truth you have in your life, the more love you will experience. Honest relationships with direct and effective communication are a source of increasing love and self-esteem. Many times we seek out relationships in order to protect ourselves from the truth. We have a sign up saying: 'If you don't tell me the truth, then I won't tell you the truth.' These relationships can be easy and comfortable but do no service to increasing your self-love and self-worth," Dr. Gray explains.

The first thing you need to do is have a clear idea in your own mind as to exactly what it means to tell the complete truth. You may think you already have such an idea, according to Dr. Gray, but it's quite possible you're wrong. He attributes that to something he calls the "Iceberg Effect." Just as only about one-tenth of a whole iceberg is visible above the surface of the water, by far the largest portion of your emotions remains hidden from view. "Most of the time, just a fraction of how you really feel shows to others and even to your conscious mind, while the majority of your emotions lie hidden deep inside of you. Thus, it becomes difficult to communicate the complete truth about your feelings because they remain a mystery even to you."

Whether you fully realize it or not, over a period of years you've actually taught yourself to subsume your emotions as a means of protecting your feelings—if you don't reveal your innermost thoughts, you can't be criticized or hurt. It's just much safer that way. "Unable to cope with and express the truth about your emotions," he says, "you learn to hide those feelings deep inside and hope that they just go away. Through years of rejecting and suppressing your feelings, you start to acquire the unfortunate and unhealthy habit of automatically repressing any unsafe, unacceptable, or confusing emotions. You learn only to express those feelings that won't disturb or threaten your life or others, thereby insuring safety and acceptance. You become a stranger to your own feelings. You begin to figure out in your head what to feel, rather than simply and spontaneously feeling from your heart," he says.

It is "absolutely essential to your growth" that you pinpoint where your emotions are hidden, he explains, "because to the extent that you suppress and bury your emotions, you will lose contact with who you are and what you really want. In my years of researching human emotions," he continues, "I have discovered a universal map of feelings to help you understand the maze of your emotions. When you are upset or unable to emotionally cope with a given situation, you are subconsciously experiencing various levels of feelings at the same time. These levels are: anger, blame and resentment; hurt, sadness, and disappointment; fear and insecurity; guilt, remorse, and regret; and love, understanding, forgiveness, and desire."

As you can see, your emotional levels are multilayered and they are all present, so even though you may only be conscious of one at a time, in actuality, many levels of emotions are constantly at work influencing how you are feeling. "If all of these levels can be fully experienced and expressed, the emotional upsets can be easily resolved. Each emotion must be fully experienced and expressed for the successful completion of the process—if not, the feelings around any upset will never be fully resolved and will most likely be repressed inside of you, creating more emotional baggage for you to carry around from relationship to relationship," he cautions.

But you open yourself back up to your partner's affection and connection when you give voice to your anxieties and release your bad feelings. "Most communication problems stem from only communicating part of the truth," Dr. Gray explains. "and not expressing the complete truth. Often when people tell the truth, they leave out many of the feelings they are having and focus on one of the above levels, excluding the others. Underneath all negative emotions are positive emotions—underneath all anger and hurt is a feeling of love and a willingness to connect and be close. The people who make you the most angry are the people you care about the most. When something someone does interferes with your ability to love that person, the first four levels of emotion will be activated. The problem arises when you communicate the anger or hurt and neglect to express the complete truth about the love underneath."

If it's "love and desire for connection" that you're looking for within yourself, then look for it "underneath all negative emotions." You need to "experience and express all those other emotions piled up on top" because that's "the only way to uncover that love," he says. "Failure to feel and express all our feelings prevents us from tapping into the vast emotional resources of love and confidence within our hearts."

By failing to get in touch with your emotions and adequately and fully express them, you run a serious risk of finding yourself trapped within emotions you actually no longer have. It's a condition Dr. Gray calls "getting stuck," and it results from an "inability to recognize and express the full range of feeling." This "will cause you to stay stuck at one level of emotion and prevent you from fully feeling your positive emotions." It could mean getting "stuck in being angry even when you didn't want to be angry anymore," or it could mean feeling "stuck in feeling sad, hurt, or depressed," and unable to shake "that gloomy feeling," or it could just leave you feeling "frozen with fear" that, in spite of your best efforts, you just can't overcome.

We all have felt pressure to live up to certain expectations by suppressing certain emotions, especially when we're young, Dr. Gray opines. "We are all taught in various direct or indirect ways not to express all of the feelings inside. Little boys are taught: 'Big boys don't cry—be strong.' The message is that they don't have to be aggressive because that's supposedly masculine. In many cases they are taught that they can't show their anger but that it isn't safe for them to show hurt or fear, for other boys might make fun of them or beat them up."

That kind of conditioning can have unintended consequences, affecting behavior later in life. For example a man who has been told through boyhood to live up to masculine expectations may, when he encounters strong feelings, "tend to get stuck on the level of anger and blame since it isn't safe for him to express the other more vulnerable levels. Often men will stay stuck in their angry feelings until they get even or until they repress the feelings entirely and shut down, becoming unreachable. I have worked with innumerable men who, when given permission to express their hurt, fear, and guilt, experienced a tremendous emotional and physical release, letting go of the anger and feeling the love again. All family violence is the result of unresolved anger," he asserts.

Repression is such a powerful thing. Have you ever known a man who seemed to be totally unconcerned and maybe even aloof when presented with a threatening situation? It could very well be that he in fact was feeling afraid or hurt, Dr. Gray says, but just couldn't admit that he was vulnerable. So while he gave every outward appearance of being calm, inside he was really angry and frustrated—certainly not a healthy situation. "Staying angry is one of the more popular ways of resisting our hurt and sadness," he relates. "The angriest people I know are the ones who have the most hurt inside. The louder they scream and yell, the longer and harder they would cry if only they'd give themselves a chance. If you get angry more than you would like to, you need to learn to cry again."

Women, on the other hand, experience exactly the opposite sort of conditioning, he points out. "Little girls are generally taught never to express anger and hostility. It's not nice to get angry or scream—Daddy won't like it, and neither will other men. Many women are taught that they can display vulnerability. They can cry all they want to, and are even programmed to feel afraid. So as an adult, when a woman has something painful happen to her, she will tend to cry and feel afraid but probably will not overtly express her anger. Crying or criticism becomes a cover-up for anger and rage. And because that rage can't come up and the woman is stuck in her sadness, she may eventually become hysterical. I've worked with countless women who felt stuck in grief and hurt. After teaching them how to express anger, I've watched them miraculously recover and feel alive, loving, and less critical."

It's so important that you learn to overcome this kind of conditioning, that you allow yourself to open up and let your anger out so long as you do it in a way that is not harmful to others or yourself. Otherwise, Dr. Gray warns, "you may be walking around afraid, hopeless, or depressed most of the time. Depression is not intense sadness," he informs, "it is suppressed anger that has been redirected at yourself. Depressed people usually feel tired and lifeless because they are using up their vital energy to keep that anger and rage from coming out." A deep depression needs to be addressed by working on "healing your old relationships, first by expressing your anger for others, then your anger at yourself, working your way back through all the other emotional levels until you arrive at the love and forgiveness," he advises.

Though he's dubious about exactly how essential communication is to a relationship, John Gottman does feel that it's important for couples to develop a "culture" all their own. For instance, in *The Seven Principles for Making Marriage Work*, he talks about a husband and wife whose successful marriage is based in part on the mutual positive image they have of themselves as "a great team." Creating your own culture "doesn't mean a couple sees eye to eye on every aspect of their life's philosophy," he explains. "Instead, there is a meshing. They find a way of honoring each other's dreams even if they don't always share them. The culture that they develop together incorporates both of their dreams. And it is flexible enough to change as husband and wife grow and develop. When a marriage has this shared sense of meaning, conflict is much less intense and perpetual problems are unlikely to lead to gridlock."

If the partners in a relationship can communicate their individual feelings to each other in an atmosphere of mutual understanding, they don't necessarily have to agree on everything all the time. "It is certainly possible," Dr. Gottman writes, "to have a stable marriage without sharing a deep sense of what is meaningful about your lives together. Your marriage can 'work' even if your dreams aren't in sync." Developing give-and-take strategies which make allowances for your inherent differences will enable you "to navigate your way around perpetual problems so that you can live with them rather than ending up gridlocked. It is important to accept that you each will probably have some dreams that the other doesn't share but can respect. You may, for example, adhere to different religions but have enough respect for each other's spiritual journey to bridge the differences in your faiths."

That's not to say, however, that your differences should be swept under the rug or just simply avoided. Quite the opposite, and that's where effective communication becomes important. As long as you are both coming from the same fundamental place, both have as your basis the mindset that you are members of the same "team," then "the richer, more meaningful, and in a sense easier your marriage is likely to be," Dr. Gottman says. "You certainly can't force yourselves to have the same deeply held views. But some coming together on these issues is likely to occur naturally if you are open to each other's perspectives. A crucial goal of any marriage, therefore, is to create an atmosphere that encourages each person to talk honestly about his or her convictions." If you both will conduct your conversations with each other in a candid and respectful manner, he writes, you will greatly increase the chances that there will be "a blending of your sense of meaning."

Most important, show your partner in your words and deeds that you place them first above all others, for "loyalty," Dr. Gottman says, "is one of the backbones of marriage and family life."

He points to a couple he has worked with in his practice whose longstanding marriage is grounded in a mutual regard for each other's family traditions and stories. Their conversations often concern "values like loyalty and generosity that had been instilled in them by hearing family stories as children. Over time, they heard each other's family stories and passed them on to their children, each other's stories became their stories too—the stories of the new family that they had created," he relates.

The message here is that "the more shared meaning you can find, the deeper, richer, and more rewarding your relationship will be. Along the way, you'll also be strengthening your marital friendship," he says. "This in turn will make it even easier to cope with any conflicts that crop up."

As we saw in the previous chapter, Dr. Gottman likes to give couples a set of questions which they can ask themselves as a means of measuring where their relationship is in certain key areas. To see how well you two are connecting through your shared rituals, he suggests you ask whether you:

"See eye to eye about the rituals that involve family dinnertimes in our home,"

Feel the same way about special occasions or holidays, whether you both think they are "special and happy times" or both dread them,

Consider "end-of-the day reunions in our home" to be "generally special times,"

"See eye to eye about the role of TV in our home,"

Think "bedtimes are generally good times for being close,"

"Do a lot of things together that we enjoy and value" on weekends,

"Have the same values about entertaining in our home" such as hosting friends, having parties, and the like,

"Both value, or both dislike special celebrations (like birthdays, anniversaries, family reunions),"

"Feel taken care of and loved by my spouse" when you are ill,

"Really look forward to and enjoy our vacations and the travel we do together,"

Think that "spending our morning time together is special to us,"

"Generally have a good time" when you perform errands together,

"Have ways of becoming renewed and refreshed when we are burned out or fatigued."

Obviously, the more yeses you can give to these questions, the stronger your marital connection is, but Dr. Gottman feels that it would take at least ten nos before you would really need to consider taking steps to shore up your relationship in this area.

If that were to be the case though, you might want to try an exercise which he says would help you establish the type of personal "culture" he talked about as being a strength for many relationships. He suggests that you have a conversation where you talk about any family rituals you each had when you were growing up. For example, share your memories of the kinds of things your families did at mealtimes and bedtimes, on weekends, during vacations, at holidays, and during illnesses. Then talk about establishing new rituals of your own, based on what you liked or disliked about your respective families' practices. Select a holiday that you both have in common and ask yourselves: "What is the true meaning of this holiday to us? How should it be celebrated this year?"

He recommends that when you agree on a ritual or set of rituals, that you write out a set protocol for them "so you will know who is expected to do what and when." Pick the types of rituals that will inspire you to "get refreshed and renewed" and that will be "something you do regularly and can look forward to."

These rituals can be as elaborate or simple as you want to make them, Dr. Gottman relates. He gives as an example a "tradition of after-dinner coffee" that the sociologist William Doherty and his wife, Leah, established "in which their children played or did homework while he and his wife had coffee and talked. They all cleaned up after dinner, then Bill made coffee and brought it out to Leah in the living room. It was a time of peace and connection."

Other possibilities would be:

"A weekly date for the two of you, away from the children.

"Celebrations of triumph—ways of celebrating almost any minor or major achievement and creating a culture of pride and praise in your marriage.

"Rituals surrounding bad luck, setbacks, fatigue, or exhaustion. How can you support, heal, and renew yourselves?

"Community rituals for entertaining friends, caring for other people in your community, or opening your home to others you care about.

"Rituals surrounding lovemaking and talking about it. These are important events that get left till the very end of the day when everyone is exhausted. Couples often think that lovemaking should be spontaneous and don't want to plan for it. But if you think about when sex is at its best, usually it's during courtship. Those romantic dates were planned, down to what to wear, what perfume or cologne to use, where to go, the music and wine after dinner, and so on. So you need to plan for romance and sex. A ritual that makes you feel emotionally safe in talking about what is good and what needs improvement in lovemaking can be very helpful.

"Rituals for keeping in touch with relatives and friends. Family events and reunions can be planned.

"Birthdays and special events that recur. Examples are holidays of importance to you, religious celebration cycles, and anniversaries.

"There are also important rites of passage that can be discussed, such as confirmations, bat mitzvahs, graduations, and weddings."

This kind of communication then, can set up the framework for a stronger relationship. Just going through the process will bring you closer together, and then the rituals you set up will reinforce and perpetuate that closeness.

CHAPTER 4

OVERCOMING CONFLICT

T he goal of good communication in a relationship is to develop more love and joy and reduce stress and conflict so that you have a better quality of life. That's a great ideal and, as we saw in the previous chapter, there are some effective and creative ways of making that happen. It's important to remember though, that it's a goal that simply isn't achievable 100 percent of the time. In fact, conflict, though certainly not something to seek out or provoke, is a completely natural part of a relationship. It's pretty safe to say that in a relationship, conflict is going to happen. Indeed, it would be a bit strange if it didn't. In this chapter, we'll take a look at workable strategies that will help you keep the number and intensity of the conflicts in your relationship to a minimum and get something positive out of them when they do occur.

Get something positive out of them? That last part may sound funny, but not only is conflict normal, it can actually play a constructive role in your relationship. "It's normal for a couple to quarrel from time to time—just part of what it means to be together," author/commentator Preston Ni, whom we met in chapter 1, says in an article on the *Psychology Today* website. "Conflicts and arguments won't necessarily jeopardize a relationship. In fact, there are times when disagreements can actually bring a couple closer together. The key is in how you and your partner decide to handle the conflict," he writes.

"Couples with poor conflict resolution skills typically engage in Fight, Flight, or Freeze behaviors. They fight and stay mad, sometimes holding grudges for years. They flee and avoid important issues by sweeping them under the rug. Or," he adds, "after endless arguments with no resolution in sight, they freeze emotionally and shut down. Someone who freezes in a relationship typically goes through the motions on the outside, but has stopped caring on the inside."

One of the big lessons couples like that could learn from those who have more stable relationships is that when an issue becomes too contentious, the best course of action sometimes is simply to "let it go." Couples in successful relationships "have the ability to solve problems," Ni says. "They focus on taking care of the issue rather than attacking the person. Even when angry, they find ways to be upset and stay close at the same time. Once the matter is resolved, they forgive and forget. Most importantly, successful couples have the ability to learn and grow through their interpersonal difficulties. Like fine wine, their relationship improves with age and gets better over time."

Ni relates the story of the time he watched an elderly couple in a coffee shop take an incident that could have caused anger and recrimination and instead gracefully turn it into a small vignette of their enduring love. He writes: "The husband accidentally knocked a cup of water over the table and onto his wife. As he got up to get some napkins, his wife announced to everyone: 'He's been doing this to me for twenty-three years!' And as the husband gently cleaned off the spill on his wife, he turned to us and said: 'She deserves it!' His wife laughed. We all laughed."

It's that knack for not letting difficulties get blown out of proportion that is so important to a long-lasting relationship. "The group with whom I've always been most fascinated is the one I call 'marital masters'—folks who are so good at handling conflict that they make marital squabbles look like fun," Ni quotes John Gottman as saying. "It's not that these couples don't get mad and disagree. It's that when they disagree, they're able to stay connected and engaged with each other. Rather than becoming defensive and hurtful, they pepper their disputes with flashes of affection, intense interest, and mutual respect," Ni quotes Dr. Gottman as saying.

Ni also cites a quote from Leo Baubauta, who advises: "Let the little things go. People who struggle often fight over little things. We obsess over things that don't really matter. We create resistance instead of letting things glide off us. Let the little things go, breathe, and move on to the important things."

Therapist and author Jamie Turndorf notes that while anger and conflict are often thought of as being the same thing, they are not. Both are a normal part of relationships and while conflict is often accompanied by anger, it need not necessarily be so, and in fact, it's vital to a working relationship that anger be kept separate and under control as much as possible. In her article, "How to Fight Right," posted on the *Psychology Today* website, the internationally recognized emotional communication expert, media therapist, and advice columnist, writes, "When it comes to conflict resolution, anger is like an accelerant. The more angry you become, the more your conflict ignites, thereby extinguishing any hope of resolution."

Many people equate anger with action, and therefore it "is anathema to conflict resolution," she says. "By this I mean, the vast majority of the human race hasn't learned to control their impulses and channel negative feelings into constructive communications. Rather, it's common for people to 'act out' angry feelings with hostile words (sarcasm, threats, yelling, name calling) or hostile behavior (slamming doors, pushing, shoving, etc.). My method is all about guiding you to not deliver raw, angry emotions in pure form to your partner."

Dr. Turndorf is the author of the book, *Kiss Your Fights Goodbye: Dr. Love's 10 Simple Steps to Cooling Conflict* and *Rekindling Your Connection,* in which she outlines "the various dysfunctional ways

MINDFUL ROMANCE: FIGHT LESS . . . LOVE MORE—TONY O'DONNELL

that people act out their anger using what I call Fight Traps. I divide Fight Traps into two categories: Open Warfare and Secret Warfare. Both types of Fight Traps throw oil on the fire and create greater relationship conflict," she explains.

"Open Warfare consists of those outright slaps in the face. These tactics are designed to hurt or pay back the person you are angry with. Open Warfare Fight Traps include: Name-Calling, Verbal Insults, Character Assassinations, I Told You So, Bringing up Ancient History, and many more."

Not as obvious but every bit as potent is "Secret Warfare," she continues. "Secret Warfare tactics include: Silent Treatment, Passive Aggression, (coming late, forgetting, withholding, etc.), Indirect Digs, Paybacks, and so on.

"Because Fight Traps are the kiss of death to your relationship, if you wish to resolve conflicts and experience harmonious loving relationships with friends and loved ones, you need to identify each and every Fight Trap that you use and permanently ditch them."

Good advice that may be, but Dr. Turndorf acknowledges that it can be very difficult to put into practice. The reason is that emotional outbursts are something that just comes naturally to a great many people. It's a reflexive habit that's very hard to break. "There is a sick satisfaction that most humans derive when they dump anger on somebody else, especially a loved one who has really hurt and angered them," she relates.

"While getting your emotional rocks off may make you feel better in the moment, on the rocks is where your relationship is going to end up. This is because emotional venting has a negative effect on the person who is being dumped on. The dumpee stores up resentment and pays you back in spades. So, whatever you say or do in the heat of the moment boomerangs back on you, meaning if you hurt your partner you are ultimately hurting yourself. By the way, beware of any form of counseling that encourages you and your partner to take turns dumping or venting on each other. Doing so only makes matters worse!"

She disagrees with the conventional wisdom that it's good to let your anger out. "Contrary to what you may have heard," she writes, "angry feelings must never ever be 'expressed.' Expressed anger refers to various forms of acting out in which one vents, rants, and raves. Expressing consists of releasing raw impulses and basically dumping on the other. The key point here is the distinction between expressing versus describing one's feelings. Describing involves taking emotional distance, and using your intellect to devise a clear-headed description of what you're feeling and why. Describing is what you're after," she opines.

"Don't fool yourself into believing that you cannot control what you say or do in the heat of anger. You can! You can control yourself when it comes to a boss or superior. You wouldn't think of telling off your boss because you know you'd lose your job! This means that you can choose to control yourself in your personal relationships if you want to. The reason people don't control themselves in their intimate relationships is because they don't think they have to. What I'm talking about here is making the choice to control yourself with those you love most, because you have to. If you don't, you won't lose your job, you'll lose your relationships."

Using the colorful imagery of a sieve, Dr. Turndorf suggests that before you communicate your thoughts to your partner, friend, or family member, use your intellect as though it were a filter and separate out those raw emotions which, if given voice, could be hurtful or damaging. In other words, if, rather than telling off the person who has made you angry, you instead take a moment and run your thoughts through your intellectual "sieve," you'll catch the "yucky emotional guck," keeping it to yourself, and your comments will be "transformed and detoxified" and become something that's "fit for human consumption."

Tell yourself that starting today, you will "only say what you know will be helpful, beneficial, and constructive not only to yourself, but also to the other party and your relationship (which is synonymous with being helpful and constructive to yourself since, as I said, everything you say and do boomerangs back on you!)," she advises.

"Keep practicing this exercise in self-discipline and you will become more and more skilled. Soon your relationship will become yet another pebble in the universal pond, a model that guides others on how to behave when they're angry. In so doing, you will not only improve your life and relationships, you will actually be instrumental in assisting the entire human race to evolve. Think of how the world would be a better place if everyone followed this principle!" Dr. Turndorf declares.

A powerful tool for keeping that anger in check is understanding where it comes from so that we can anticipate what types of situations are likely to trigger it and thus we are ready do deal with it and defuse it. Not surprisingly, many of the conflicts between partners are firmly grounded in basic differences in how men and women view relationships. It turns out that men and women are often looking for different things in a relationship and have very different expectations for how their partner should behave and respond to their actions. For some background on this, we turn to Dr. Emerson Eggerichs whose book, *Love and Respect*, contains some valuable insights into male-female relations.

Most men feel disrespected, states the president of Love and Respect Ministries, which is dedicated to building healthy marriages. In a national survey conducted by Decision Analysts, Inc., he notes, 81.5 percent of the male participants said that the statement, "My wife doesn't respect me right now," accurately describes how they feel when they are in the midst of an argument with their partner.

"The survey substantiated what I had already discovered in my years of working with married couples: Men need to feel respected during conflict more than they need to feel loved. This does not mean men do not need love. Men know deep down that their wives love them, but they are not at all sure that their wives respect them. During marital conflict it is clear that men place a higher value on feeling respected than feeling loved. Many women cannot imagine this because they are still tuned in to the love wavelength. Practically every woman I have met or counseled would be willing to say, 'I just want somebody to love me, to make me special, to make me the most important one in his life.' Now no one seizes on these words and accuses women of being prima donnas or egomaniacs, yet when a man says he needs to be respected, he's often labeled, especially in our culture, as arrogant."

To fully appreciate how important a woman's expressions of respect and admiration can be to a man, "just go back to your days of courting," he writes. "During courtships, the woman may have thought that her man was motivated to ask her to marry him because of her love. After all, love is what motivated her, in fact, her love was huge, there is no question about that. But more than she ever realized, it was her unique and intimate admiration that won her man's heart. The old saying puts it, 'Every man does what he does for the admiration of one woman.' Back in courtship days, she became that woman and he bowed the knee and proposed. He felt deep feelings of love for her, but they came out of his being convinced that she respected him and admired him for who he was. She was striking a chord deep within him that literally drove his life then as it drives his life today."

For most men, Dr. Eggerichs believes, honor and respect hold equal value. "My experience as a man and with other men tells me that in our arena we have an honor code and if we don't live by that honor code we're in big trouble. We've learned from boyhood that there are certain things you just don't do, certain things you just don't say. A woman will talk to a husband in the home in a way that a man would never talk to him. He can't believe that she can be so belligerent, so disrespectful. The husband will often look away, wanting to drop the argument and move on. He doesn't want to talk about it. Why? Because he feels engulfed and overpowered by his wife's dark countenance, negative emotions, and combative words. All this annoys and incites him so he withdraws. To him, that is the honorable thing to do."

Take a look at your own situation, he suggests, and reflect on whether you are a criticizer or a stonewaller. "According to John Gottman's extensive research, 85 percent of husbands eventually stonewall their wives during conflict. For a man, tension builds much faster because his blood pressure and his heart rate rise much higher and stay elevated much longer than his wife's. During tense exchanges, a wife's negative criticism can overwhelm the husband and he has little appetite to deal with it. The wife sees such exchanges as potentially increasing the love between them, and her heartbeats per minute (BPM) do not escalate. The husband on the other hand, sees the exchange as an argument in which he is is apt to lose respect, and this revs up his BPMs. In an attempt to calm himself down, the husband will stonewall, become quiet, say nothing, or go off by himself. If asked why he is stonewalling, the husband will say something like, 'I'm trying not to react, I'm just trying to calm myself down.' "

What looks to the woman like stonewalling, which she regards as unloving, however, looks very different to the man, Dr. Eggerichs says. To him "he is simply trying to do the honorable and respectable thing. But his wife thinks he is rejecting her. How could he possibly want to withdraw and stonewall her when all she has done is given him a minor criticism or two?" Dr. Eggerichs quotes Dr. Gottman: "Such interactions can create a vicious cycle, especially in marriage with high levels of conflict. The more wives complain and criticize, the more husbands withdraw and stonewall. The more husbands withdraw and stonewall, the more wives complain and criticize." Dr. Eggerichs adds that Dr. Gottman says that if a wife becomes belligerent and contemptuous, the marriage is in serious danger, and if this cycle isn't broken, it will probably end in divorce.

In most relationships, "the wives are usually the ones who are the criticizers, the confronters, the ones who want to get things out on the table and get them settled," Dr. Eggerichs says. "There are wives who stonewall at times, but in my experience, they are in the minority. My view is that when a wife does stonewall, she does so because she has lost confidence that her husband will hear her heart. She longs to connect, but has given up hope. While his heart rate may be going through the roof, hers is slow and steady because her heart is broken."

"In the majority of cases, a wife who is in love with her husband will move towards him when she feels unloved. For example, it's the first year of marriage and he's been late to dinner two nights in a row without calling. She says to herself, 'This is wrong. How can he be so insensitive? Am I last on his priority list? This is so unloving.' Instinctively, she proceeds to say what she believes is the loving thing when he comes through the door: 'We need to talk, we need to talk right now. Please sit down and talk to me.' In approaching her husband in this fashion, the wife is using the same approach she would use with a best girlfriend.

"When women have conflicts with each other, they both usually verbalize their feelings. They share what is on their hearts because instinctively they know it will eventually lead to reconciliation. At some point, one of them will say, 'Well, I was wrong,' then the other will say, 'No I was wrong too. Will you forgive me?' and the other will say, 'Yes, of course I'll forgive you, but you know, I'm really sorry.' Then they hug, shed a few tears, and pretty soon they're laughing. That's what I call bringing things full circle."

But while this routine can be very effective in relationships between women, it's often exactly the wrong thing to do in male-female pairings, Dr. Eggerichs says. "Unfortunately, women think this approach will work with their husbands just as well as it does with their best girlfriends. When a problem arises and something feels unloving, the wife instinctively moves toward her husband to share her feelings. Her eventual goal is that both of them will apologize and then embrace. This is the way she keeps her marriage up to date, a high value for her. Her heart longs to resolve things and reconcile. Her husband matters more to her than any adult on earth. In truth, her confrontation is a compliment. She thinks, 'Oh that he could see my heart. Why does he close himself off from me?'"

The mistake many women make, he explains, is to think that her relationship with her husband or significant other is like her relationship with her best girlfriend. "What a wife usually fails to see is that a big difference exists between her best girlfriend and her husband. A wife will be more judgmental toward her husband than toward her best girlfriend. She feels free to do this because as his loving helpmate, part of her mission in her mind is to help change him into a loving man. She knows that if she can just get her criticism out on the table, he can change. And if he'll change to be a bit more loving, she knows she will out-love him," he writes.

"A wife's self image may depend on her husband's approval," he continues. "The typical wife also fails to realize that her self-image often rests on what she believes her husband thinks of her. This is not the case with a girlfriend. Her girlfriend's opinion of her is important, but not as vital as her husband's opinion. Also, the marriage relationship, unlike her relationship to a girlfriend, is a topic of ongoing discussion between her and other women. Women want to report to each other how wonderful their marriages are. So a wife's negativity can intensify when her husband stonewalls her efforts to get him to change. He isn't making her feel good, and she can't report to her friends the joys of her marriage. If her negativity intensifies, she is in danger of becoming even more belligerent and contemptuous and then her husband will close her off completely. Proverbs 21:19 says: 'It is better to live in a desert land than with a contentious and vexing woman.'"

54

The ironic thing is, her acting that way oftentimes is her response to what is in fact a misinterpretation of her by her husband. "He doesn't decipher the code in which she cries, 'I need your love.' Instead he hears, 'I don't respect you.' This sweet, tender, godly woman is misunderstood. When she gets too negative, she does herself and her marriage no favors. Thankfully, some women are becoming aware that negative confrontation doesn't work. As one wife said, 'My strength and verbal skills aren't helping my marriage. I've come across to my husband as too strong and too controlling and too critical. I've been his mommy and his teacher and his holy spirit. It's my own personal nature to lead and direct and control and fix and do right and make others do the same. He is scared of my tongue.' "

When a wife is too blunt in telling her husband what she feels he is doing wrong and how she thinks he should correct it, many times it can trigger what Dr. Eggerichs terms as the "crazy cycle"—a seemingly endless loop of complaints and recriminations between them. "When a man begins to feel that his wife no longer looks up to him but is looking down at him, the crazy cycle kicks in. The crazy cycle often starts when women start scolding in the home. The word 'scold' is often associated with mothers balling out their children. The dictionary definition however, says that scolding means to reprimand or criticize harshly and usually angrily and even openly."

Feelings of annoyance and being disrespected are the inevitable reaction in husbands whose wives confront them with "repeated reprimands and scolding," he writes. "Wives, however, tend not to see this. When a wife scolds her husband, she's only trying to help correct things, keep things on an even keel. And there's no doubt at times men need this kind of help. But when a man begins to feel that what his wife is saying reduces him to a child being scolded, there can be trouble. He doesn't necessarily see his wife's heart, he only hears her words, which are saying that she's looking down on him. To paraphrase Proverbs, he would rather live in the wilderness than with this irritating woman. While many wives do not intend to be disrespectful, it would appear that way to their husbands, and their husbands take refuge in stonewalling them."

Dr. Eggerichs says he has queried many businessmen for their opinion on this subject, asking them, "Do you want your associates to love you or respect you?" Invariably their reaction is one of surprise and amusement: "I could care less if they love me," they will typically say, laughing, "but respect me? Absolutely," he reports. The take-away message seems to be, "Right or wrong, men interpret their world through the respect grid, and a wife's softened tone and facial expressions can do more for her marriage than she can imagine."

Sometimes challenging a person's actions can simply be a matter of helping them view those actions from a different perspective, Dr. Eggerichs says. For example, he will often ask a female client to think about how she is treating her husband and then to reflect on how she would feel if a woman was treating her son that way. He says when he puts it in those terms, they are chagrined at their behavior. "It is high time for women to start discovering how their husbands really feel. One woman was shocked when she asked her husband, 'Do you want me to tell you that I love you or that I respect you?' Without hesitation he replied, 'Respect.' She couldn't believe her ears. She had never realized that though he needed her love, what he lacked was assurance of her respect."

It can be a hard lesson for many women to learn, he says. "I'm sorry that they have to feel everything from amazement to shame. No one is trying to shame wives. On the contrary, our respect message is designed to help wives see that their big, powerful husbands are really in need of something that wives can give: respect. When a husband receives unconditional respect from his wife, those fond feelings of affection and love return, and he will start giving her the kind of love she has always hoped to receive."

Why is this such a sticking point? Because men and women tend to define respect and love quite differently, he explains. "There are many wives who tell me, 'Respect and love are the same thing.' I respond, 'No they aren't and you know they aren't. For instance, you respect your boss, you don't love your boss. I've been in counseling sessions with couples and with her mate sitting right there next to her the wife will readily say, 'I love my husband but don't feel any respect for him.'"

He continues, "But when I turn this around, and ask the women how they would feel if they hear their husband say, 'I respect you but I don't love you,' they are horrified. They explain, 'I would be devastated!' I asked one woman, 'How long would it take you to get over that?' She quickly answered, 'Forever!' The typical wife would be up in arms if she heard, 'I respect you but don't love you.' That is taboo. She would view her husband as a very unloving human being. Yet this same wife feels she can readily say to him, 'I love you but don't respect you.' What she doesn't understand is that her husband is equally devastated by her comment, and that it also takes him forever to get over it. The bottom line is that husbands and wives need to feel that they are truly equal. She needs unconditional love and he needs unconditional respect."

Conflict is inevitable in any relationship between two distinct individuals, but not all conflicts are created equal. Some are more serious than others, and it's helpful to distinguish between them. "Some conflicts are minor irritants, but others can seem overwhelmingly complex and intense," John Gottman explains in his Seven Principles. "Too often couples feel mired in conflict or have distanced themselves from each other as a protective device."

Dr. Gottman notes that his extensive research shows "that all marital conflicts, ranging from mundane annoyances to all-out wars, really fall into one of two categories: Either they can be resolved or they are perpetual, which means they will be part of your lives forever, in some form or another. Once you are able to identify and define your various disagreements, you'll be able to customize your coping strategies, depending on which of these two types of conflict you're having."

The bad news is that after careful analysis of the data, he has come to the conclusion that nearly 70 percent of marital issues qualify as perpetual problems. "Time and again when we do four-year follow-ups of couples, we find that they are still arguing about precisely the same issue," he reveals. "It's as if four minutes have passed rather than four years. They've donned new clothes, altered their hairstyles, and gained (or lost) a few pounds and wrinkles, but they're still having the same argument."

Such ongoing disagreements could be, as he has observed, over such things as a wife who wants kids but the husband who doesn't or the husband who would like to have sex more often than the wife or the spouse who is constantly after the other for not doing their fair share of the housework or the husband who wants to rear their children in a religious faith different from the wife's or the couple who can't agree on the proper amount of discipline for their children.

Instances of irreconcilable conflicts it would seem, right? Actually, no, Dr. Gottman reports. "Despite their differences, these couples remain very satisfied with their marriages because they have hit upon a way to deal with their unbudgeable problem so it doesn't overwhelm them. They've learned to keep it in its place and to have a sense of humor about it." One couple he has counseled calmly discusses the problem with him without getting angry, recounting their conversations about it in a good-natured manner, complete with impressions of each other. The problem still exists for them, "but they've learned to live with it and approach it with good humor." The point is, "despite what many therapists will tell you, you don't have to resolve your major marital conflicts for your marriage to thrive."

Conflicts "are inevitably part of a relationship much the way chronic physical ailments are inevitable as you get older. They are like a trick knee, a bad back, an irritable bowel, or tennis elbow. We may not love these problems, but we are able to cope with them, to avoid situations that worsen them, and to develop strategies and routines that help us deal with them. Psychologist Dan Wile said it best in his book, *After The Honeymoon*: 'When choosing a long-term partner . . . you will inevitably be choosing a particular set of unsolvable problems that you'll be grappling with for the next ten, twenty, or fifty years.'" Adding his own comment, Dr. Gottman remarks, "Marriages are successful to the degree that the problems you choose are the ones you can cope with."

Failed marriages aren't necessarily those with fewer problems, they're the ones where the husband and wife allow their relationship to become "gridlocked" and die because they haven't made enough effort to work out creative ways of dealing with their perpetual problems. "They have the same conversation about it over and over again," he writes. "They just spin their wheels, resolving nothing. Because they make no headway, they feel increasingly hurt, ever more present when they argue, while humor and affection become less so. They become all the more entrenched in their positions. Gradually they feel physiologically overwhelmed. They start a slow process of trying to isolate or enclose this problem area. But actually they have started becoming emotionally disengaged from each other. They are on the course toward parallel lives and inevitable loneliness—the death knell of any marriage."

Recognizing that it's not always easy to identify those perpetual problems which have become so intractable that they have you gridlocked, Dr. Gottman suggests that couples consider whether: "the conflict makes you feel rejected by your partner; you keep talking about it but make no headway; you become entrenched in your positions and are unwilling to budge; when you discuss the subject, you end up feeling more frustrated and hurt; your conversations about the problem are devoid of humor, amusement, or affection; you become even more unbudgeable over time, which leads you to vilify each other during these conversations; this vilification makes you all the more rooted in your position and polarized, more extreme in your view, and all the less willing to compromise; (and) eventually, you disengage from each other emotionally."

If these are "painfully familiar" descriptions of your issues, "take comfort in knowing that there is a way out of gridlock, no matter how entrenched in it you are," he reassures couples. "All you need is motivation and willingness to explore the hidden issues that are really causing the gridlock. The key will be to uncover and share with each other the significant personal dreams you have for your life. I have found that unrequited dreams are at the core of every gridlocked conflict. In other words, the endless argument symbolizes some profound difference between you that needs to be addressed before you can put the problem in its place."

Although solvable problems are, by definition, not as intrenched as the perpetual kind, Dr. Gottman cautions couples not to underestimate them. "These problems may sound relatively simple compared with unsolvable ones, but they can cause a great deal of pain between husband and wife. Just because a problem is solvable doesn't mean it gets resolved. When a solvable problem causes excessive tension, it's because the couple haven't learned effective techniques for conquering it. They aren't to blame—far too many of the conflict resolution ideas recommended by marriage manuals and therapists are not easy to master or apply. Most of these strategies focus on validating your partner's perspective and learning to be a good listener. There's nothing wrong with this—except that it's very hard for most people to do at any time, much less when they're distressed."

So what is a solvable problem? "One way to identify solvable problems," he suggests, "is that they seem less painful, gut-wrenching, or intense than perpetual, gridlocked ones. That's because when you argue over a solvable problem, your focus is only on a particular dilemma or situation. There is no underlying conflict that's fueling your dispute." Such arguments can even be about the same thing, the only difference being the thinking behind them. For instance, a dispute where a wife nags a husband about getting the garbage ready ahead of time is solvable if she's doing it because they missed the truck the previous week. It becomes perpetual if what's behind it is her feeling that he is sloppy and disorganized and his feeling that she is controlling and doesn't respect him.

"The basis for coping effectively with either kind of problem is the same: communicating basic acceptance of your partner's personality. Human nature dictates that is is virtually impossible to accept advice from someone unless you feel that that person understands you. So the bottom-line rule is that, before you ask your partner to change the way he or she drives, eats, or makes love, you must make your partner feel that you are understanding. If either (or both) of you feels judged, misunderstood, or rejected by the other, you will not be able to manage the problems in your marriage. This holds for big problems and small ones."

In any dispute, the most important thing is not what you say but what you hear. In fact, "you may discover that your partner is more conciliatory during arguments than you realized—once you know what to listen for," he says. Take our hypothetical garbage dispute. If she says, "You got the garbage out too late last week, you're always procrastinating. You never get anything done on time," you can put that argument down in the unsolvable column. But if she says, "Phew, that garbage from last week stinks! Let's be sure we get it out there before the truck comes this time," there's a much higher likelihood that the problem will be solved (and there'll maybe even be a laugh about it).

"Maybe that second approach takes a bit longer. But that extra time is worth it since it is the only approach that works. It's just a fact that people can change only if they feel that they are basically liked and accepted as they are," Dr. Gottman advises. "When people feel criticized, disliked, and unappreciated, they are unable to change. Instead, they feel under siege and dig in to protect themselves."

Research has shown "that the key to instilling in children a positive self-image and effective social skills is to communicate to them that we understand their feelings," he relates. Adults would be wise to take that lesson to heart in their own world. "Children grow and change optimally when we acknowledge their emotions ('That doggie scared you,' 'You're crying because you're sad right now,' 'You sound very angry. Let's talk about it.') rather than belittle or punish them for their feelings ('It's silly to be afraid of such a little dog,' 'Big boys don't cry,' 'No angry bears allowed in this house—go to your room till you calm down.'). When you let a child know that his or her feelings are okay to have, you are also communicating that the child himself or herself is acceptable even when sad or crabby or scared. This helps the child to feel good about himself or herself, which makes positive growth and change possible. The same is true for adults. In order to improve a marriage, we need to feel accepted by our spouse."

He adds, "Another important lesson I have learned is that in all arguments, both solvable and perpetual, no one is ever right. There is no absolute reality in marital conflict, only two subjective realities."

That's great advice. Be sensitive to your partner's point of view and realize that neither one of you has all the answers. Make the most of the mindfulness we talked about in chapter 1 and the power of communication that we saw in chapter 2. When things get tough, as they will, hang in there. Breathe. Stick with it. Talk it over. In later chapters of this book we'll look at the importance of owing up to it when you are wrong and saying you are sorry, and other strategies that will enable you to patch things up in your relationship before it's too late.

Sometimes, though, before that kind of reconciliation can happen there has to be a break, a brief time out. When things get too intense—when the "crazy cycle," as Dr. Eggerichs calls it, gets spinning too fast—the best thing to do is simply give it all a rest and go your own way for a little while. Taking a time out can be effective, but it has to be done the right way, and that's what we'll be looking at in the next chapter.

CHAPTER 5

CHOOSING FLIGHT OVER FIGHT: SOMETIMES YOU NEED TO WALK AWAY (FOR AWHILE)

Clearly, calm, reasoned discussion is the most desirable course for resolving conflicts in a relationship. But sometimes the atmosphere is simply too charged with emotion to allow for such constructive exchanges between partners. Too often we will find ourselves saying and even doing things when we're highly agitated that we would never do otherwise. Nothing good or useful is going to come out of it when the screaming and yelling starts, and in fact, at that point you are at risk of having things escalate out of control.

Before something happens that you'll regret later, it's crucial that at least one of you takes a stand and says, "You know what? I want to hear what you have to say, but perhaps this is not the right time right now because I feel that both of us are very emotional, both of us seem like we're out of control, and we're not really listening and paying attention to each other. Can we revisit this in an hour? I just want to let you know that I'm going for a walk, or I'm going for a coffee, or I'm going to ride my bicycle, or I'm going to go work out at the gym." We need to be sure that we don't simply walk out the door without saying anything. We need to let our partners know where we're going and that we'll be right back after we've had a little break so they feel secure. Once you've said where you're going and for how long though, it's time to just walk away without further confrontation.

And when I say walk away, I don't mean walk away and leave the relationship. If the struggle or the argument is getting too heated, it's important to do a time-out and let your partner know that this is too much, you can't handle this right now. In the heat of passion, men and women will tend to follow each other into different rooms and carry on the argument until they become incredibly upset and before they know it, they're flinging things at each other and saying things that are verbally abusive and extremely hurtful to one another. It's important that you don't let it get to that level.

Do it right, announce your intentions, but don't delay. It's important that you appreciate that the quicker you walk away, the more you save face and preserve an opportunity to come back and reconnect again. If things start to escalate in the first couple of minutes of the argument, don't let it go further. You need to be able to have the tools in order to do so, but remind the person that you're going to be right back. You need to take a break. Tell your partner, "I don't want to hurt you by saying something that I will regret later and I just want to let you know that I need to take a break, I'm going for a walk, and I'll be right back in twenty minutes or thirty minutes, whatever. I'm sorry, this is not working for me right now. I don't want to say something that hurts or offends you. I'm going to come right back in about thirty minutes to an hour. I'll just be right down the road. I have my cell phone with me if you need to call me. Is that O.K. with you?"

A conversation may still continue to escalate, but just keep reminding them, "I need to take a break" and walk towards the door and back away, so the further you back away from the argument, the more you lessen the intensity and as a result, you lower their stress levels. Women want to get their stuff out, men want to get their stuff out, and everyone wants to be heard. The reason that we fight in the first place is because we're so misunderstood. We just lack the tools in order to communicate effectively and as a result, we have misunderstandings, we have arguments, we have conflicts, and we have unnecessary fights that could be reduced simply if we just listened to each other. So back away as quickly as possible. When an argument escalates to a level that may get out of control we need to retreat and apologize without delay. Then when we return we can effect a change in his or her behavior because once the person is understood and hears what you're saying, conflict is reduced dramatically.

"Sometimes, not talking is more effective" than trying to reason things out, agrees John Gray. In his book, *Why Mars and Venus Collide*, he writes, "When tension arises between men and women, one of the most important skills is to take time-out."

Most times it should be the man who takes the initiative to break things off when the argument gets too heated, he feels. Men's "hormones are already designed for fight or flight. Under stress, a woman is designed to talk more. When tension begins to build and voices are raised, the best choice is to postpone having the conversation until both people have a chance to calm down and feel good again," he says.

"During a time-out, he should do something he loves, and she should talk with someone other than her partner. This is very important. Sometimes when men walk away, women will follow and continue to ask questions. This only makes matters worse. A man should not under any circumstances answer those questions. He should simply walk away. If he needs to say something, he should only repeat what he said to initiate the time-out."

When you declare your intentions, you should do it with as "polite and non-inflammatory" words as possible, he suggests. Instead of saying something like,

—"You are being irrational. I can't talk with you,"

Dr. Gray proposes that you say,

—"You have a right to be upset. Let me think about what you have said and then let's talk more about this."

Rather than using a dismissive phrase such as,

—"This is a complete waste of my time. I can't talk with you,"

he proposes a more conciliatory approach like,

—"What you say is important to me. I need some time to think about this and then we can talk."

Don't say,

—"I can't take this anymore. You are so stubborn," he counsels.

Instead say,

—"I want to talk about this, and I need more time to think about it. Let's talk more about this later."

Something like,

—"You don't hear a word I say. Nobody can talk with you" will get you nowhere.

Much better would be,

—"You are right. Let me think about this and then let's talk about this for a moment."

He advises against making it all about you with a statement such as,

—"I am out of here. I will not take this kind of abuse."

Vastly better would be a declaration that takes both your feelings into consideration, like,

—"I can appreciate what you are saying. I need some time to think about my response. Let's talk more about this later."

A comment such as,

—"I feel so hurt that you would say that. I can't believe this. I have nothing to say to you," not only isn't going to defuse the confrontation, it's only going to make matters worse.

Dr. Gray allows that it would be more beneficial to say something short and to the point like,

—"You are being mean. I need some time to think about this, and then we can talk."

Even though the time-out concept comes more naturally to a man, he says, women often come to appreciate its value when they have experienced it a few times. "Since she is not from Mars, how can she know when her feelings are pushing him over the edge, enraging him and making him aggressive? But ultimately, it is not her responsibility to protect him. He needs to protect her and their relationship. By taking a time-out, he is protecting her from the warrior within whose only alternative to flight is to fight."

Although "a woman should recognize that she can't say whatever she wants regardless of his sensitivities," Dr. Gray writes, "she should not feel as if she has to walk on eggshells around him. In the name of honesty, both men and women are too quick to give up the virtues of patience, flexibility, and the consideration of another's feelings and sensitivities."

It will often happen that a woman will be caught completely off guard by her partner's violent reaction because she's totally clueless as to the effect her remarks have on him, he explains. "If he doesn't take responsibility to let her know he is reaching the combustion point by taking a time-out, she becomes accustomed to his angry response and can be afraid to bring up her needs and wishes. A man is actually making it safe for her to talk by taking a time-out when he has heard too much or they are heading down the wrong road."

Given her natural proclivity for dealing with stressful situations by talking things out, taking a time-out is a harder course of action for a woman, he says. "Talking almost always works on Venus, but not on Mars. On Venus, it is even against the law to walk away in the middle of a conversation. Without a common understanding and acceptance of taking time-outs, a woman can become offended and even more upset when a man takes a time-out."

The fact that a woman's "hormones under stress are so different" from a man's means that she "does not recognize the importance of taking a time-out," he relates. "For her, talking about something and being heard, making a connection, will stimulate oxytocin and lower her stress levels. Her natural tendency is to talk more at these times. What she does not grasp is that talking can sometimes intensify her partner's frustration and anger," he says, likening it to "pouring gas on the fire" of his already raging emotions. "If he feels she is making him out to be in the wrong or trying to control him, he can get angrier and more upset."

This doesn't mean a woman shouldn't follow her natural desire to talk things out, it just means she should seek out an appropriate audience for what she has to say. It definitely shouldn't be her partner and it usually shouldn't even be a family member. That's because much of what she will be saying pertains only to the moment—to the specific disagreement at hand—and doesn't reflect the full range feelings she has for her partner. "Talking with family members can come back to haunt you," Dr. Gray cautions. "They hold on to all the negative feelings you may temporarily have about your partner. They are not aware of all the positive feelings you have toward your partner to hold a healthy balance. Confiding in family members at your worst moments may drive a wedge between them and your partner."

Much more suitable choices for auditors would be "a friend, a therapist, a relationship coach, or a support group of other women," he offers, further suggesting that the woman "write her feelings in a journal, or . . . pray. In these ways, she can gradually explore her emotions, sorting out her thoughts to identify her needs and positive feelings. With more positive feelings and a clear awareness of what she needs, she is better equipped to communicate her perspective and hear what he has to say. A couple should wait at least twelve hours before discussing the issue again."

Keeping in mind that "men are from Mars," he says, the woman should consider that "she may be misinterpreting his actions or words. During this time, she can reflect on ways she can view or talk about the situation or conflict in a more positive manner. Sometimes remembering the good things he does can soften her feelings. It can be helpful to present her point of view to herself or a friend in a more positive manner that doesn't reject him but acknowledges the support he does provide."

He suggests a dozen questions that a woman should pose to herself prior to resuming her discussion of the issue with her partner:

"What am I blaming him for?

"What am I angry about, sad about, or afraid of?

"What do I expect him to say, do, or feel?

"Are my expectations reasonable?

"What do I really need?

"How is he misinterpreting me?

"How could I be misinterpreting him?

"What do I regret?

What do I trust, accept, or appreciate about him?

"What do I forgive him for?

"What would I like him to say or do?"

For his part, a man "should first do what he needs to feel better and then reflect on a better way to communicate with his partner," Dr. Gray advises. "For him, this is a different process. He needs to do a testosterone-producing activity that he enjoys, like playing solitaire online, watching a game, or reading the newspaper. After he feels better, he can reflect on what they were talking about, so that he can clearly express his thoughts and desires after hearing what she has to say."

The man should replay the argument in his head, right down to the actual words that were said, he suggests, and then "reflect on what was not said that should have been said." Echoing Dr. Gottman's admonition in the previous chapter that "in all arguments . . . no one is ever right. There is no absolute reality in marital conflict, only two subjective realities," Dr. Gray writes that the man "should take a critical look first at what she did wrong and then at what he did wrong. This kind of thinking puts him in the problem-solving mode, which will always make a man feel better and make him a better communicator."

The man "can consider what she needed and how she could have said it in a way that would make him feel more appreciated," he proposes. "Doing this helps him to understand that it is not always an easy task to say things in ways that don't bother him. He can think about how he probably made the conversation worse by trying to fix her or solve the problem before taking the time to hear her. This process tends to soften his heart and to take away his defensiveness."

And as with the dozen questions Dr. Gray suggested women consider, he offers twelve things he feels men should think about before they attempt to revisit the contentious issue that led to the time-out:

"What did she say that was annoying?

"What did she not say that she should have said?

"What was she trying to say?

"How could she have said it differently?

"What did she need?

"How is she misinterpreting me?

"How could I be misinterpreting her?

"What is the best possible outcome for each of us?

"What do I regret, or how should I have done it differently?

"What do I forgive her for?

"What would I like her to say or do?"

Analyzing where the situation went awry and achieving a definitive mental image of the steps to reconciliation are crucial for the male way of thinking, showing him the way forward, Dr. Gray says. "Men can quickly resolve their feelings if they can create a clear picture in their minds of what happened that didn't work, and what will work. There are millions of factors in our lives that affect our mood and temperament. When your partner is upset or defensive, it doesn't matter how reasonable or legitimate your perspective is. Nothing you say or do will help. You must accept that for a period of time neither of you can hear, understand, or appreciate the other's point of view. At these times, there is nothing you can do but retreat and try again later, but not before a twelve-hour break." Or, as they say on "Mars": "When a tornado comes, find a ditch and lie low."

Once a couple adopts taking time-outs as a regular routine for preventing arguments from going ballistic, it becomes part of a category of strategies that Dr. Gottman calls "a repair attempt." These are strategies that the partners in a relationship agree to follow and can count on as a fallback when the going gets tough. In this case, it's saying things like "Let's take a break," or "Wait, I need to calm down," he says in The Seven Principles for Making Marriage Work. This approach can "deescalate the tension during a touchy discussion—to put on the brakes so flooding is prevented." He uses the term, "flooding," he notes, to describe those occasions when "your spouse's negativity—whether in the guise of criticism or contempt or even defensiveness—is so overwhelming, and so sudden, that it leaves you shell-shocked." Another example of a "repair attempt" that he cites is a couple who stick their tongues out at each other to break the tension when things get too heated. A "repair attempt," he says, "refers to any statement or action—silly or otherwise—that prevents negativity from escalating out of control."

Repair attempts are the secret weapon of emotionally intelligent couples—even though many of these couples aren't aware that they are doing something so powerful. When a couple have a strong friendship, they naturally become experts at sending each other repair attempts and at correctly reading those sent their way. But when couples are in negative override, even a repair statement as blunt as 'Hey, I'm sorry' will have a low success rate."

In a similar vein, marriage and family relationships expert and psychologist Harriet Lerner suggests that couples come up with certain "anger rules" that they agree to follow during arguments. In the article, "The Secret To Stop Fighting With Your Partner," posted on the Psychology Today website, she relates the story of former clients of hers: "Years back, I saw a high powered, professional couple in San Francisco who went at each other's throats, verbally speaking, twenty-four/seven. Everything turned into an epic battle—whether the issue was eating meals, having sex, planning vacations, spending and saving money, decorating the house, rearing kids, or dealing with in-laws and ex-spouses. When they fought, they 'kitchen sinked it,' revisiting one old hurt after another and never resolving anything."

Nothing this couple had tried seemed to work, says Dr. Lerner. "Both claimed they were powerless to control their tempers. Then, a distinguished British professor came to stay with them as their houseguest for several months, living in a guest room adjacent to their bedroom. 'During that time, we never raised our voices,' the wife told me. 'We were pretty courteous with each other. Pride, I guess.' They both agreed it was the best several months of their marriage."

It would be nice to have "a distinguished British houseguest to loan out to my high-conflict clients," the author of *The Dance of Anger* writes in the *Psychology Today* article. "It might be a useful exercise to imagine that you have one of your own. I certainly could have used one during those times in my marriage when I just cut loose. Like the couple in San Francisco, we might all learn that we're capable of adjusting our behavior. It's all about motivation. Most couples have more control over fighting than they think they do."

She suggests that partners "make rules for how you as a couple will treat each other. Agree to follow them even in the heat of the moment. We often act as if the intensity of our anger gives us license to say or do anything, because, after all, we're way too furious to be able to stop what's coming out of our mouth!"

The most important thing is that the rules provide for a fair fight, she says. "There's no shortage of advice from experts about how to fight fair in marriage. I suggest you begin by sitting down with your partner and coming up with a few rules of your own. These might be, for example, 'No yelling or name calling,' 'No bringing up past grievances during a fight,' 'No bringing up problems at bedtime.'

Many couples find it helpful to keep a written copy of the rules in a place where both will see it daily, like in your sock drawer," she notes.

"Happy couples are not couples that don't fight. Rather, they're couples that fight fair, and take responsibility for their own words and actions, no matter how furious they may feel inside. Of course we can stop ourselves and behave better," Dr. Lerner declares, "that is if we have a genuine intention to have a better marriage."

No matter what they call it, whether it's "anger rules" or a "repair attempt" or something else, the extent that both partners buy in to their peace-restoring strategy, Dr. Gottman asserts, will go a long way toward determining "whether their marriage flourishes or flounders. And again, what determines the success of their repair attempts is the strength of their marital friendship. . . . Strengthening your marital friendship isn't as basic as just being 'nice.' Even if you feel that your friendship is already quite solid, you may be surprised to find there is room to strengthen it all the more. Most of the couples who take our workshop are relieved to hear that almost everybody messes up during marital conflict. What matters is whether the repairs are successful."

The stakes for that success are pretty high, because an argument out of control becomes a force of nature that's almost impossible to stop. The reason for that is that it involves both emotional and physical elements, Dr. Gottman explains. "When your body goes into overdrive during an argument, it is responding to a very primitive alarm system we inherited from our prehistoric ancestors. All those distressful reactions, like a pounding heart and sweating, occur because on a fundamental level your body perceives your current situation as dangerous. Even though we live in the age of in vitro conception, organ transplants, and gene mapping, from an evolutionary standpoint not much time has passed since we were cave dwellers. So the human body has not refined its fear reactions—it responds the same way, whether you're facing a saber-toothed tiger or a contemptuous spouse demanding to know why you can never remember to put the toilet seat back down."

So no matter how valid you think your position is, if you force your opinion on your partner you can expect to be rejected every time. It's like Dr. Gray says: "If you cannot hear her point of view, don't expect her to be able to hear your point of view. As your resistance increases, so does your partner's. In this way, resistance is guaranteed to intensify."

That's the reasoning behind "another Mars/Venus ground rule to avoid fights," he explains: "He needs to hear her thoughts, feelings, and needs before she needs to hear what he has to say. Men have a greater ability to listen as long as they recognize that they are solving the problem by listening and not arguing."

Given a man's natural tendency to find solutions and a woman's inclination to talk things out, "once she has talked, his job to fix things is to communicate to her satisfaction that he has heard her point of view. If a man recognizes how important his listening is to his partner's well-being, he will be willing to do it. When her oxytocin levels rise and stress stops paralyzing her, she becomes capable of hearing what he has to say. When both feel heard, they become flexible enough to make a compromise if that is what is needed."

If a couple is to follow Dr. Gray's "Mars/Venus technique for avoiding a heated and painful fight," the time-out should be declared by the man and the initiative for resuming the discussion should come from the woman. In other words, "He calls for a retreat to regroup, and later she approaches him with a white flag to talk." By doing so, "he protects them from hurting each other by insisting on a time-out, and she helps bring them back together with conversation."

He suggests that the man call a halt to the bickering by saying, " 'Let's first just talk about how you feel, and then we can focus on problem solving later.' When they talk, he should only respond by making supportive comments like, 'Tell me more.' When she is done, he could say, 'Let me think about this, and then we can talk later about what to do.' "

It doesn't necessarily have to be the man who calls the time-out or the woman who initiates the resumption of talks, "but this suggested order is most aligned with our hormonal differences and will help reduce the stress of the situation," Dr. Gray writes.

In another article on the *Psychology Today* website, "When Fighting Gets Ugly, No Rules Apply But This One!" Dr. Lerner opines, "Ideally, partners can call an end to escalating fights before they get out of control. In real life, however, things can go from zero to one hundred before one person realizes they should have exited the conversation earlier. When an argument has degenerated into a screaming match, or one person has absorbed more emotional intensity than he or she can manage, stop the interaction immediately."

Heed your partner if they say, "leave me alone," she urges, although she notes that it's O.K. to gauge your actions to the situation at hand. "If she doesn't seem all that upset, you can offer one more invitation to keep the conversation going." You can try saying things like, "I'm sorry I was being obnoxious. Can we try that again? I promise to lower my voice," she writes, but be wary. "If your partner still wants to be left alone, force yourself to get away. This means no following her to a different room, no slipping notes under the door, no calling or texting, no adding one more word to the conversation until you've both calmed down."

Dr. Lerner suggests that "the partner who stops the fight can take the initiative to revisit the subject within twenty-four hours, unless the issue was really small and stupid, or one person hasn't calmed down. Stop rules ('leave me alone') don't work well unless each party knows they can re-open the conversation at a later time. When you've reached a certain level of intensity, no rules apply except this one," she adds. "Even pursuing your partner with the intention of clarifying your position or apologizing, is counterproductive when he or she has reached their limit. 'Leave me alone!' means 'Leave me alone!' "

In this chapter, we've seen how, when done properly, time-outs can be effective in heading off disastrous arguments, or cutting them off once they've begun. We've learned that we need to carefully state our intentions before walking out, being clear that this is only a temporary solution and that we'll revisit and try to resolve the issue later, and how crucial it is that this be done in a polite, and respectful manner. We now know also that being firm is just as important as being courteous, that once we've made the decision to take a break, and once we have let our partner know what we're doing, we need to leave quickly and not let the discussion persist.

And as we've seen, time-outs shouldn't just be a period of cooling down, they should also be about mulling over our partner's statements and opinions and reconsidering our own position. Perhaps we can find things on our partner's side that, in calm hindsight, we find reasonable and similarly, maybe there are parts of our argument that aren't as important as we thought they were in the heat of battle.

Finally, we've discovered how fundamental differences between men and women can often be the underlying source of arguments and misunderstandings, and how these differences can complicate the resolution of disputes. Some of these gender differences are ingrained in us by culture and some, as we're about to examine in the next chapter, are grounded in hormonal and other biological issues. Being aware of these differences and making allowances for them can be key to maintaining a successful relationship.

CHAPTER 6

RECOGNIZING AND DEALING WITH OUR DIFFERENCES

Hormones are so important for our overall wellbeing. They play a key role in both our physical and mental functioning. Women need time to refuel, to raise their oxytocin levels. Men need time to refuel too, but even though we both have that basic need, we do things totally differently. Women raise their oxytocin levels by going and talking to their friends or going shopping, and it makes them feel good. Men raise their testosterone levels by watching a ballgame or reading a good book or going to see a movie or hanging out with their friends and having a couple of beers. So we both need to find a balance.

John Gray defines hormones well when he explains that they "are chemical messengers that act as a catalyst for chemical changes at the cellular level that affect growth, development, energy, and mood." That's why our hormone levels have such a dramatic effect on our moods. If your hormones are out of whack, off balance, off kilter, it's not pleasant for either party in a relationship, so it's very important that you make sure that you go to a physician and have your levels checked. Once your personal levels are established, you can see what you need to do in order to effect change in your hormones. One simple way to do so that doesn't cost any money or require you take anything is to get more rest and more sleep. Research now indicates that men and women who don't sleep enough tend to experience significant hormonal imbalance. They suffer from excessive adrenal exhaustion and often are more agitated and moody as a result.

That can be highly detrimental to a relationship because hormonal imbalances can lead directly to disagreements. Many times we argue simply because we haven't eaten or we haven't had enough rest and if we're tired from not having enough rest or we haven't had proper fuel or the kids are driving us crazy or we had a bad phone call, or had a flat tire—whatever it is—you're going to be irritated and agitated as a result. Hormones control our body's chemistry, and as a result, it's important that we take care of them.

Hormonal fluctuations can cause us to gain weight. Excessively high levels of cortisone may be a root cause of our feeling moody and agitated and angry and upset at little things. Hormones are also involved when we're in love. Falling in love "stimulates a cascade of hormones that temporarily lowers stress levels," according to Dr. Gray. "When we are in love, we feel on top of the world. We are filled with energy. We are euphoric. We are ardent about our new love, and consequently we are more generous in accepting or overlooking our differences. In the early state of love, we are eager to support our partner's needs. Taking care of his partner boosts special hormones in a man, while being provided for stimulates different hormones in a woman. When these hormones are abundant at the start of a relationship, the stress, clamor, and pressure of our daily lives dissolves into the background."

The differences between men and women are hardwired into their being, he writes in *Why Mars and Venus Collide.* "The way our brains are structured and function is not the same." Certain behavioral expectations conveyed through our parents and society in general account for some of the differences while basic biological variations account for others.

There is a fundamental reality in the relationship between women and men, agrees John Gottman: "Women are more oriented toward discussing and understanding feelings than are men," he writes in *The Seven Principles For Making Marriage Work*. "I'm not suggesting that all women are savvier about emotions and have better 'people skills' than all men. There are plenty of women who are tone deaf to social nuances and insensitive to others. But usually women are more emotionally intelligent than their husbands for one simple reason: They've had an enormous head start in acquiring these skills. Observe children at any playground, and you'll see that head start in action. When young boys play (usually run-and-chase games) their priority is the game itself—not their relationship with each other and their feelings. But for little girls, feelings are paramount. A cry of 'I'm not your friend anymore' will stop a game cold. Whether it starts up again," he points out, "will depend on whether the girls make up."

The same gender difference, he relates, could be seen in the behavior of a boy and girl, both four-year-olds, whom he observed playing with a baby doll. At first the boy went along with the girl's "relationship-based play" of pretending that they were showing off their "baby" to friends, but "then the game roller-coasted into boy territory" with the boy declaring that the "baby" had died and that they needed to "get it to the hospital right away. He climbed into a pretend ambulance and away he went, 'Brrrrrrrrrr.'" The girl went along with the dramatic change in scenario, admonishing the boy to drive more carefully as they raced to the hospital, and then assuming the role of surgeon (instead of nurse, as he had intended for her—"so some things have changed!" Dr. Gottman exclaims) to save the baby's life after they arrived at the hospital. Once that was accomplished, they resumed her original storyline of introducing the "child" to their friends.

In his analysis of the play session, Dr. Gottman states that although the children's imaginings were "equally charming and delightful," the "plain truth" of such activity "is that 'girlish' games offer far better preparation for marriage and family life because they focus on relationships. As a general rule, boys don't even include games with relationship and domestic themes in their repertoire. Think about it: While no preschool dress-up corner would be complete without bridal costumes, you never see tuxedos for little pretend grooms!"

This fact prompts him to wonder, "Where does this difference in play styles between boys and girls originate? Because it occurs in virtually every culture, I suspect that it is caused mostly by biology rather than socialization. But whether nature or nurture is the cause of these differences, their effect is undeniable. Because their play emphasizes social interactions and feelings, girls undergo an extensive education into emotions by childhood's end. Boys learn how to pitch overhand. A boy's experience at playing cooperatively and quickly resolving conflicts will be an asset later in the boardroom or on the construction site, but it will be a liability in marriage if it comes at the expense of understanding the emotions behind his wife's perspectives."

As cross-gender interaction becomes less common among older children and boys and girls reinforce their own behavioral patterns playing amongst themselves, boys become less exposed to girls' sensibilities and the gap becomes wider, he explains. "Although about 35 percent of preschool best friendships are between boys and girls," he relates, "by age seven that percentage plummets to virtually zero percent. From then till puberty the sexes will have little or nothing to do with each other. This is a worldwide phenomenon.

"Many explanations have been given for this voluntary segregation. One intriguing theory, by psychologist Eleanor Maccoby, Ph.D., at Stanford University, dovetails with my findings on accepting influence. She found that even at very young ages (one and a half years), boys will accept influence only from other boys when they play, whereas girls accept influence equally from girls or boys. At around ages five to seven, girls become fed up with this state of affairs and stop wanting to play with boys. From that age until puberty, our culture (and virtually all others) offers no formal structure for ensuring that boys and girls continue to interact."

Thus, he writes, "once a couple move in together or get engaged, the groom-to-be is suddenly immersed in what is probably an alien world." He cites a line in the Broadway play, "In Defense of the Cave Man," which is humorous and illustrative of his point: "A man says that when he was first married, he saw his wife cleaning the bathroom and asked her, 'Are we moving?'" The reason he thinks that, Dr. Gottman explains, is that in the character's "bachelor days that was the only time he bothered to clean the bathroom. Many young husbands discover they have a lot to learn from their wives about maintaining a home," he adds.

"You can see the shell-shocked look on the face of the typical young fiancé in any home furnishings store. He neither knows nor cares about the difference between taffeta and chintz. All of the china and silver patterns look remarkably alike to him. Most of all he's thinking that this is taking an awfully long time, and if he turns around suddenly he will do about $10,000 worth of damage since all of the shelves are made of glass and placed about two feet apart, probably just to intimidate guys like him. How will he react? If pretty soon he hears himself saying, 'Hey, that's a great pattern,' another emotionally intelligent husband has been born."

Dr. Gottman relates that his research indicates an acceleration in the number of newlywed husbands experiencing this type of alteration. "About 35 percent of the men we've studied fall into this category. Research from previous decades suggests the number used to be much lower. Because this type of husband honors and respects his wife, he will be open to learning more about emotions from her. He will come to understand her world and those of his children and friends. He may not emote in the same way that his wife does, but he will learn how to better connect with her emotionally. As he does so, he'll make choices that show he honors her. When he's watching the football game and she needs to talk, he'll turn off the TV and listen. He is choosing 'us' over 'me.'

"I believe the emotionally intelligent husband is the next step in social evolution," he continues. "This doesn't mean that he is superior to other men in personality, upbringing, or moral fiber. He has simply figured out something very important about being married that the others haven't—yet. And that is how to honor his wife and convey his respect to her. It is really that elementary."

This change in overall outlook likely will alter how this type of husband defines success and thus will inspire him to regard his career as secondary in importance to his family, Dr. Gottman surmises. In contrast to husbands of an earlier era, "he naturally . . . makes a detailed map of his wife's world. He keeps in touch with his admiration and fondness for her, and he communicates it by turning toward her in his daily actions."

Likewise, Dr. Gray feels that embracing the contrasts between the outlook of men and women is vital for both partners in a relationship because "acknowledging these hardwired gender differences helps us to identify and release our unrealistic expectations that our partners be more like us and to accept that we are not the same. At first, these differences may seem to be a hinderance, but once you fully understand the biology, it becomes clear that we complement each other perfectly. In fact, it is as if men and women were made for each other," he says.

For one thing, while the hormone, testosterone, is primarily associated with men, the fact is that both men and women produce it, it's just that men produce far more—up to thirty times more—than women. Early in a relationship is one of the prime times for testosterone production in a man, as the challenge of gaining a woman's attention raises his excitement levels. Dr. Gray describes testosterone as "the hormone from Mars that contributes to a man's sense of power and well-being. When his testosterone levels are at normal levels, he is pumped and is more attentive and attracted to his partner."

One of the things testosterone does for a person—and women are particularly sensitive to its effects—is give "you a sense of youthfulness because it helps your body maintain muscle mass, bone density, optimal lipid profiles, and levels of red blood cells," he explains. By the age of thirty, though, the gradual decline in testosterone begins which in men "can lead to decreased sex drive, erectile dysfunction, depressed mood, and difficulties with concentration and memory."

A condition known as "irritable male syndrome" has been identified by scientists, "characterized by withdrawal, irritability, and depression. A new study has found that levels of testosterone of men in the United States have been falling steadily during the past twenty years," he reports. It's actually something of a mystery, because "factors such as aging, smoking, and obesity do not fully explain the decline. A diet high in meat and poultry might contribute to the downward trend, because the hormones used in meat production act like estrogen in the body. Estrogen, the female sex hormone, inhibits the production of testosterone. Alcohol and soy products also have a negative effect on testosterone levels. Beer, for example, contains plant estrogens that can eventually reduce testosterone levels, one of the reasons intoxication and sex sometimes do not mix."

A variety of approaches to boost testosterone levels through creams, gels, or patches are employed by many men in an effort to counteract this decline. In fact, in 2011 sales of prescription measures aimed at increasing testosterone—estimated at 5.3 million— were five times what they were just ten years before, according to U.S. Food and Drug Administration figures.

The trouble is, Dr. Gray points out, that "the body is not designed to take hormones. When you take a hormone, it will give you symptomatic relief for a while, but there are side effects. If you take hormones, your body gradually loses its ability to make those hormones over time. Besides altering your natural hormone production and a long list of other side effects, new research is showing that this type of testosterone therapy may increase your risk of dying from a sudden stroke or heart attack by 29 percent, regardless of whether you had underlying coronary heart disease or not," he warns. In fact, the connection is of such a concern that "a recent randomized clinical trial of testosterone therapy in men with a high prevalence of cardiovascular diseases was stopped prematurely due to adverse cardiovascular events."

Another complication is that no individual man is exactly the same in terms of how much testosterone their body needs for proper lean body mass, strength, and sexual function, Dr. Gray says. "When you take synthetic testosterone, you are supplying your body with an arbitrary dose of testosterone hormone that is thought to be ideal for men. It makes more sense to allow your body to normalize its own testosterone levels, based on what it needs for optimal health."

He recommends "focusing your efforts on healthy lifestyle strategies, rather than taking synthetic hormone replacement, because the risk of taking synthetic testosterone is still largely unknown. There are a number of things a man (or woman) can do to boost testosterone levels naturally." He recommends making "some dietary and exercise changes, particularly by limiting sugar and fructose, doing high-intensity exercises, and supplementing with Eurycoma Longifolia Jack." Also known as Tongkat Ali, Eurycoma Longifolia Jack "derives from a plant and it helps increase testosterone production in your body. This all-natural herb is not a testosterone replacement, nor does it directly increase testosterone. Instead, it activates your body's ability to make testosterone."

He reports that "Tongkat Ali is traditionally prescribed in Malaysia as an aphrodisiac and as a treatment for sexual dysfunction. Tongkat Ali seems to not only assist in maintaining erections but it also has been known to increase the libido and sexual desire in women. It also enhances energy levels, endurance, and stamina, and reduces occasional mental fatigue. For the greatest impact," Dr. Gray asserts, "nutritional supplementation should be combined with exercise of short intervals of high intensity exertion followed by periods of rest. This is what your body is hardwired for and it emulates the daily physical actions and movements of ancient man."

The short exercise intervals should be of ten to fifteen minutes' duration, he suggests, noting that while a slow one-hour jog or brisk walk is an excellent workout for the lungs and heart, it does not have the needed effect for boosting testosterone production. "Clearly, low testosterone is not an inevitable fate for aging men," he writes on his blog, marsvenus.com, "and you don't have to risk your health by experimenting with synthetic hormones in order to maintain youthful levels. Even if you believe the risks to your heart are small (although I personally would not consider a nearly 30 percent increased risk to be negligible), I encourage you to consider the big picture. Using exercise and diet will allow your body to optimize testosterone and other hormones to levels that are ideal for you. By opting for hormone therapy as your first line of treatment, you're cheating yourself out of most, if not all, of those benefits—and you may even end up doing more harm than good."

Oxytocin, which Dr. Gray calls "the cuddle hormone," is primarily associated with women, but just like testosterone, it is produced by both sexes. Also "known as a social attachment hormone," oxytocin is produced by women in large amounts during childbirth and when they are lactating, while both men and women produce it during orgasm. Women can produce oxytocin in response to various stimuli such as massage, while emotions such as a feeling of neglect can actually cause a decrease in the amount of oxytocin in a woman's system.

He relates that "social recognition and bonding as well as the formulation of trust between people" are all affected by oxytocin. Both "maternal behavior and sexual arousal" are stimulated in women by oxytocin, he says, adding, "it reduces blood pressure, cortisone levels, and fear. Studies have shown that animals and people with high levels of oxytocin are calmer, less anxious, and more social."

Unlike testosterone, which as we saw is present in significantly larger amounts in men than in women, oxytocin levels tend to be about the same in both sexes, Dr. Gray explains. The difference is that the potency of oxytocin is enhanced by estrogen, which women do have in larger quantities than men. The disparity in effective levels of oxytocin in men and women is further widened by the fact that oxytocin is suppressed by testosterone.

He refers to oxytocin as "the cuddle hormone" because it "creates a feeling of attachment. Levels increase when women connect with someone through friendship, sharing, caring, and nurturing, and decrease when a woman misses someone or experiences a loss or breakup or feels alone, ignored, rejected, unsupported, and insignificant. A woman in love has high levels of oxytocin. She is consumed by thoughts of giving freely of herself and sharing more time with her partner."

As a result of this biological process, "a woman needs to trust that her partner cares for her as much as she cares for him," he explains. "This kind of support directly affects her oxytocin levels, which in turn will lower her stress. Messages from him of caring, understanding, and respect can build trust and nourish her soul while stimulating higher levels of oxytocin.

In fact, a woman's perception of a wide range of her partner's actions and attitudes can have a direct impact on her oxytocin levels: "How she interprets his behavior makes all the difference," he continues. "If she interprets his behavior as caring for her, then her oxytocin levels go up, but if she interprets the same behavior as not caring, her oxytocin levels go down."

So much depends on whether her expectations of his conduct are met or whether they are disappointed. "Trust in her relationships and the anticipation of getting her needs met as she meets the needs of her partner fuel the rise of a woman's oxytocin levels. This positive anticipation is reversed when a woman expects more from a man than he can provide. Her disappointment restricts the production of oxytocin," he relates.

A woman's oxytocin levels can be inhibited if she sets the bar too high. "Instead of looking to other sources of support, she expects her partner to do it all. By expecting her partner to be the main source of stimulation to produce oxytocin, she is setting her partner up to fail."

It doesn't have to be that way, he points out, noting that woman can look elsewhere for oxytocin level-raising stimuli. "A woman's oxytocin levels rise when she is helping someone, because she cares about that person and not because she is getting paid or because it is her job. When we give primarily to get, that causes testosterone, not oxytocin, to rise. When women begin to feel they are not getting enough in their relationships, they tend to give to their partner with strings. They give, but become more concerned about what they are getting or not getting in return. This kind of result-oriented giving does not stimulate as much oxytocin, because it is tinged with negativity and anger. Unconditional giving is a powerful oxytocin producer. Oxytocin levels go up when we are caring, sharing, and befriending without expectations. Just as oxytocin production increases when we are nurturing to others, it is also stimulated when we are nurturing to ourselves."

Some of the activities Dr. Gray cites as "oxytocin stimulators" are: sharing, communicating, being safe, cleaning, grooming, trusting, working as part of a team, caring, sharing responsibility, being consistent, giving compliments, showing affection, being virtuous, nurturing, being supportive, cooperating with others, collaborating with others, participating in group efforts, and following a regular routine.

When a woman "feels free to nurture herself or others" in her home or in her relationships with others, her body will produce oxytocin, he says. But her reserves of stress-reducing oxytocin will be drained "when she feels rushed, overwhelmed, or pressured to do everything," and so her level of stress will thus be raised. In that event, in order for her oxytocin levels to be restored, she'll need to feel listened-to, acknowledged, and cared for. "At the end of the day, the anticipation of a simple hug, conversation, and some affection can make a big difference on Venus. When a woman thinks she can't get what she needs at home, her warm feelings dissipate, and her oxytocin levels fall," Dr. Gray writes.

That can lead directly into "the Crazy Cycle" that Emerson Eggerichs talks about and which we first encountered in Chapter 4. "Getting on the Crazy Cycle is all too easy," he writes in *Love & Respect.* "Recognizing that you're on the Crazy Cycle and learning how to keep it from spinning out of control is possible if husband and wife can learn how to meet each other's basic needs for love and respect. I have often been asked, 'How can you be so sure the wife primarily needs to feel love and the husband primarily needs to feel respect?' My answer comes in two parts."

For one thing, Dr. Eggerichs reports, the truth of the statement regarding these basic needs has been borne out repeatedly in his professional experiences as a counselor and his personal experiences as a husband. "The wife is the one who asks, 'Does my husband love me as much as I love him?' She knows she loves him, but she wonders at times if he loves her nearly as much. So when he comes across as unloving, she typically reacts in a negative way. In her opinion, he needs to change into a more sensitive and caring man. Unfortunately, a wife's usual approach is to complain and criticize in order to motivate her husband to become more loving. This usually proves about as successful as trying to sell brass knuckles to Mother Teresa," he quips.

"On the other hand, a husband does not commonly ask, 'Does my wife love me as much as I love her?' Why not? Because he is assured of her love. I often ask husbands, 'Does your wife love you?' They reply, 'Yes, of course.' But then I ask, 'Does she like you?' And the answer usually comes back, 'Nope.'"

So even though they feel their relationship is based on love, this type of husband still worries that deep down, his wife harbors disrespectful and even contemptuous feelings toward him. "In his opinion, she has changed from being the admiring, ever-approving woman she was when they courted. Now she doesn't approve, and she's letting him know it. So the husband decides he will motivate his wife to become more respectful by acting in unloving ways. This usually proves about as successful as trying to sell a pickup to an Amish farmer," he remarks.

Dr. Eggerichs further backs up his assertion with the lessons found in the Bible, citing Ephesians 5:33 which "teaches about the woman's primary need for love and the man's primary need for respect: The husband must love his wife as he loves himself, and the wife must respect her husband. Could it be any clearer than that?" he asks. "Paul isn't making suggestions: he is issuing commands from God Himself. In addition, the Greek word Paul uses for love in this verse is agape, meaning unconditional love. And the wording of the rest of the passage strongly suggests that the husband should receive unconditional respect. Christian spouses should not read this verse to say, 'Husbands, love your wives unconditionally, and wives, respect your husbands only if they have earned and deserve it.' As the old saying goes, what is sauce for the goose, is sauce for the gander. In this verse, respect for the husband is just as important as love for the wife."

Turning to another passage of Scripture, 1 Peter 3:1–2, Dr. Eggerichs notes Peter also weighed in on the matter, telling "wives that if any husbands were disobedient to God's Word, 'they may be won without a word by the behavior of their wives, as they observe your chaste and respectful behavior.' Peter is definitely talking about unconditional respect. The husbands he mentions are either carnal Christians or unbelievers who are disobedient to the Word—that is, to Jesus Christ. God is not pleased with a man like this, and such a man does not 'deserve' his wife's respect. But Peter is not calling on wives to feel respect; he is commanding them to show respectful behavior. This is not about the husband deserving respect; it is about the wife being willing to treat her husband respectfully without conditions."

Acting against your natural inclinations is certainly not something people would normally be expected to do, Dr. Eggerichs acknowledges, so as a result, "this passage must be acted on in faith. God has ordained that wives respect their husbands as a method to win husbands to Himself. As a husband opens his spirit to God, he reopens his spirit to his wife. No husband feels affection toward a wife who appears to have contempt for who he is as a human being. The key to creating fond feelings of love in a husband toward his wife is through showing him unconditional respect."

Dr. Eggerichs says he has been bolstered in his determination to make the need for respect central to his theories on building successful relationships by the response he and his wife, Sarah, have gotten from the "thousands of married couples" they have encountered in their seminars. He says that "again and again, we receive confirmation that we are definitely on the right track. Every wife we've met wants her husband to appreciate how much she loves him, and she yearns to feel more love from him. What we try to share is that the best way to love a husband is to show him respect in ways that are meaningful to him. Such respect lets him feel his wife's love for him and ignites in him feelings of love for his wife."

The arguments proposed by Dr. Eggerichs add a spiritual dimension to the physical and emotional components so vital to our relations with our partner and provide another path for us to conduct ourselves in ways that show sensitivity to the needs we each have.

We must strive to appreciate the ways we are similar and the ways we are not and make allowances in our approach to our relationship.

For Dr. Gottman, it's all about making adjustments to cultural changes that have gradually been taking place over the past several decades in the male-female relationship. Some men are comfortable keeping up with the times and have embraced these changing roles. "This new type of husband and father leads a meaningful and rich life. Having a happy family base makes it possible for him to create and work effectively. Because he is so connected to his wife, she will come to him not only when she is troubled but when she is delighted. When the city awakens to a beautiful fresh snowstorm, his children will come running for him to see it. The people who matter most to him will care about him when he lives and mourn him when he dies."

Other men have been unwilling to give up what they regard as their privileged status as the undisputed leader and decision maker in the relationship, accountable only to their own beliefs, whims, and desires. Some of the men who have clung to this archaic concept of the husband's absolute supremacy have wound up being sorry for it. This type of man "responds to the loss of male entitlement with righteous indignation, or he feels like an innocent victim. He may become more authoritarian or withdraw into a lonely shell, protecting what little he has left. He does not give others very much honor and respect," Dr. Gottman declares. "He fears any further loss of power. And because he will not accept influence, he will not have very much influence. The consequence is that no-one will much care about him when he lives nor mourn him when he dies."

However counterproductive this stubbornness may be, it is somewhat understandable because this shift in marital relations and sharing of power is still a relatively new phenomenon, coming amidst a sea change of societal alterations which have occurred gradually over just the past several decades. Many men can recall a much different situation with their fathers and grandfathers. And after all, "for centuries men were expected to be in charge of their families," he writes. "That sense of responsibility and entitlement gets passed down from father to son in so many subtle ways that revising the husband's role can be a challenge for many men."

The "lord and master" type of mindset we're talking about is neatly summed up in a passage from Robert K. Massie's monumental biography, Catherine the Great, in which Catherine's teenaged future husband, Peter, receives this guidance from one of his servants as to Peter's proper role in the relationship: "The husband must be the master. The wife should not speak in his presence without his permission, and only a donkey would allow a wife to have opinions of her own. If there was trouble, a few well-timed knocks on the head would put things right." How did that work out for Peter? Not too well, really, as he suffered from poor health while Catherine went on to become a strong ruler of the sprawling empire, well deserving of the appellation, "The Great."

Consciously or unconsciously, more and more men are now are embracing their new sensitivity to their wives' desires and needs, and if that "sounds like a feminist line," Dr. Gottman allows, "it's also the reality. With more than 60 percent of married women working, the male's role as the sole breadwinner is on the wane. Increasingly women's jobs provide them with a source not only of income and economic power but of self-esteem as well. A significant number of the core issues we see between couples today have to do with this change in gender roles. Often wives complain that men still aren't doing their fair share of domestic chores and child care."

Rather than being limited to young couples, Dr. Gottman says, his research shows that the issue is a sticking point for older couples even into their sixties as well. "Men who are willing to accept influence are happily married. Those who are not see their marriages become unstable. As one unhappy husband put it, 'I married June

Cleaver and she turned into Murphy Brown. It's not fair. I didn't bargain for this.' "

Another reason men may balk at accepting this change is that they may feel it's a movement that won't last. Dr. Gottman advises against that attitude. "There is scientific evidence that we are living through a cultural transformation that will not come undone. Anthropologist Peggy Sanday, Ph.D., a professor at the University of Pennsylvania, has devoted her career to studying and comparing hunter-gatherer cultures all over the world. On the surface our lives may seem very different from those of the peoples she studies. But human nature is fundamentally the same. Sanday has identified certain factors that determine whether a culture will be male dominant or egalitarian. (Interestingly, no cultures were female dominant.) She has also studied the signs that a culture is moving in one direction or the other."

Dr. Sanday's research, Dr. Gottman reports, finds that a society may be defined as male dominated if it contains the following characteristics:

- A scarcity of food resulting in difficult day-to-day living and environmental dangers;
- A perception that meat from large game animals has greater value than any other food source;
- A culture in which the care and raising of infants is left entirely to women, with men's roles being limited to occasionally caring for children;
- A near absence of female figures in the sacred symbols of the culture's creation myths and other sacred symbols.

Her studies indicated that the more these characteristics prevail in a society, the more male dominant these cultures tend to be, according to Dr. Gottman. "And when these factors moved in the opposite direction, the culture also shifted to an egalitarian mode where men and women shared power," he relates. "I believe you can see such a change happening in our culture today," he asserts, pointing to the prevalence of the following factors:

- An abundant food supply and an environment considerably safer than that of many generations ago, maintained by laws which "keep the bulk of people feeling relatively safe;"
- The rising number of women who are "the sole breadwinners or 'hunters' for food;"
- The increasing desire of fathers "to participate in the care and raising of infants" as evidenced by "an explosion in the number of men who attend childbirth classes with their wives, are present at the birth of their children, and share in the diapering, feeding, and bathing of their babies." Further evidence of this can be observed at practically any park, where "you're likely to see young fathers carrying Snuglis and pushing strollers." Although "many women feel that men still don't do enough caretaking of the very young," he notes, "it's clear there's been a shift in attitude;"
- "An increasingly strong female representation in our culture's sacred symbols. Catholicism has seen an important growth in worship involving Mary, the mother of Christ," he says. "Not only has worship increasingly involved Mary, but her role has shifted dramatically from being the passive recipient of the Hold Spirit to being a woman who bravely and actively chooses to accept the role of mother in her encounter with the angel Gabriel (Luke 1:26–38). She intercedes on behalf of supplicants with love, compassion, and understanding," he relates.

Both conservative and reform movements within Judaism "have rewritten prayer books to emphasize the female in the sacred. The importance of the matriarchs is recognized, as well as the Shechi-nah, the female qualities of God: forgiveness, compassion, under-standing and love."

Of course, the trend is not yet universal and may never be. But more and more, men "are seeking guidance in coping with the cul-tural change," Dr. Gottman maintains. "Witness the growing popu-larity of organized men's movements such as the Promise Keepers, the Robert Bly mythopoetic movement, the Million Man March, and the men's rights movement. People are now marching on Wash-ington not to demand political change but to make new vows about their role in families. Whatever your opinion of each of these groups, their very existence is a symptom of the seismic shift in so-cial relations that has left many men lost and befuddled."

Individually, men must "decide how to deal with this great trans-formation," he writes. "Our research clearly indicates that the only effective approach is to embrace the change rather than to react with anger and hostility. Time and again we can separate the happy from the unstable couples based on whether the husband is willing to ac-cept influence from his wife."

He likens those men who fight the trend to a motorist who en-counters "frustrating bottlenecks and unexpected barricades" as they negotiate the streets of an unfamiliar city. "You can take one of two approaches to these impossible situations. One is to stop, be-come righteously indignant, and insist that the offending obstacle move. The other is to drive around it. The first approach will even-tually earn you a heart attack. The second approach—which I call yielding to win—will get you home."

The perennial issue of the tipped-up toilet seat provides a "clas-sic example" of a yielding-to-win strategy, Dr. Gottman says. "The typical woman gets irritated when her husband leaves the toilet seat up, even though it only takes her a millisecond to put it down her-self. For many women, a raised toilet seat is symbolic of the male's sense of entitlement. So a man can score major points with his wife just by putting the seat down. The wise husband smiles at how smart he is as he drops the lid."

A willingness to compromise is the key to resolving relationship conflicts, he says. "You do this by searching through your partner's request for something you can relinquish." An example he gives of a good compromise involves a husband who has been scheduled to work extra hours and thus will not be home when his wife's mother visits, much to the irritation of his wife. A possible solution to this situation would be for the husband to schedule his work for Saturday morning when he normally takes his son to soccer practice, thus allowing him to help his wife prepare for her mother's stay the night before. Then on Saturday, the wife and her mother could take the son to soccer.

If you are the type of man who has a hard time accepting his wife's influence and making such compromises, you can at least "acknowledge the problem and talk with your spouse about it," Dr. Gottman advises. "Nobody can change old habits overnight. But if you're able to take responsibility for the parts o your marital troubles that are caused by your difficulty with sharing power, that in itself will be a major leap forward for your marriage. Your spouse is likely to feel a great sense of relief and renewed optimism about improving your marriage. The next step is to make your partner an ally in your crusade to overcome this problem. Ask her (or him) to gently point out to you instances where you are being unwittingly domineering, defensive, or disrespectful."

The more you talk things through and the more you try little compromises "the more skilled you become at accepting influence" he writes. "A willingness to share power and to respect the other person's view is a prerequisite of compromising. For that reason, becoming more adept at accepting influence will help you cope far better with marital conflict."

It's all about respecting each other for who we are and frankly recognizing how we are different and how we are similar. As Dr. Gray says, "If we cannot find a way to embrace the differences and to achieve a balance, sustaining a relationship is difficult. Many couples never develop their relationships beyond dating. Others make a commitment, but over time, their differences erode their intimacy, and they split up. In these instances, both believe that there was not enough common ground for the relationship to work. Though sometimes couples are not compatible, usually their problems derive from not understanding their differences."

Dr. Gray imagines how some of those misunderstandings might sound when expressed by the two partners:

> The woman might say things like: "He was just too stubborn to change;" "He was so self-centered. He wasn't even interested in my life or my feelings;" "He became so cold and detached. I didn't feel safe to open up with him;" "I used to be number one, but as soon as he got me, work became his number-one priority;" "He never listens to what I say. All he wants to do is solve my problems;" "He was afraid of intimacy. Every time we would get closer, he would pull away;" "Everything started out fine, and then he changed."
>
> Conversely, the man's comments might run like this: "She used to appreciate everything I did, but gradually she wanted to change me;" "She was too needy. Everything was about her;" "Everything was about her feelings. I felt completely controlled;" "Gradually, the kids became more important than me;" "She gets so emotional and then makes no sense at all;" "She was so responsive in the beginning. Now I feel like I have to fill out a form before we have sex;" "She was too high-maintenance. Whatever I did, it was never enough. There was always something I did wrong."

These types of complaints, he says, are based in "a lack of understanding and acceptance of our basic differences. They are certainly legitimate complaints, but they emerge because we fail to take our differences into account."

You may be experiencing difficulty in your relationship, or may have encountered problems in the past and one or more of Dr. Gray's above imagined complaints may ring true to you as closely matching things your partner has actually said. If so, "your resistance to natural differences may be at the root of many of your collisions. When you resist rather than support your partner's needs when he or she is coping with stress, you will evoke the worst of your partner's character. If you are single, this insight might make you aware that you have alienated a potential partner or that your behavior may have been misinterpreted by another. Whether you are married or single, a new understanding and acceptance of how we are supposed to be different will enable you to bring out the best in your partner and yourself as well."

This acceptance, however, doesn't mean that anything goes. It's one thing to stop trying to change you partner's behavior, as some married couples do as a means of maintaining a smooth relationship, but it's quite another to simply accept whatever negative behavior our partner exhibits. "Instead," Dr. Gray says, "loving acceptance provides a foundation from which we can work with our differences, so that both partners get what they need most. Accepting our differences is not always easy," he allows, "especially when we are under stress," which, not coincidentally, is the subject of the next chapter.

As we've already seen in this chapter and as will be reinforced in the next, hormones are vitally important to our health and wellbeing as well as to our relationships. We've seen ways the basic differences between men and women are hardwired into our being through both cultural influence and physiological factors including the degree to which different levels of testosterone and oxytocin affect men's and women's behaviors. Awareness of this influence is crucial to our being able to understand and compensate for these differences, setting our expectations for our partners' behavior accordingly. Likewise being aware of our competing needs for love and respect is key to adjusting our actions in ways that will allow us to maintain healthy relationships. And we've seen how some relationships depend on the partners' ability to adjust to changing social standards concerning the roles of men and women.

So you have to make sure your hormone levels are balanced and that you get proper rest. Sadly, most women don't rest, don't sleep enough. You're either a workaholic or you're not. And most women that I know tend to work really hard—they're raising three, four children, sometimes more, sometimes less, they're always preparing meals, they're doing so much. We are so grateful for women because I come myself from a family of eleven back in my native Ireland. My mother worked constantly, worked on the farm, worked at making dinners, food, and preparing breakfasts and lunches and dinners, getting us off to school and making sure we got there, getting our clothes ready, making sure we were bathed and our hair was clean and our nails were clean, our bodies were clean. She did so much for so many years and so we need to show some more gratefulness for the women in our lives because where would we be without them? It's important that we honor and respect that.

In the next chapter we'll be taking an in-depth look at how relationships are affected by stress, the psychological and biological sources of stress including its effect on hormones, the consequences for our health, and options for relieving stress through natural, non-chemical means.

CHAPTER 7

STRESS: UNHEALTHY FOR OURSELVES AND OUR RELATIONSHIPS

O f all the many causes of divorce and breakups of relationships, stress is probably one of the highest on the list, with financial pressure being one of the prime sources. As I mentioned earlier in this book, with both parents working outside the home, it's often the case that they rarely get to see each other. They leave in the morning at six-thirty, seven o'clock and come home at ten, eleven o'clock at night. Both parents are working so hard.

When we're stressed, our hormone levels go out of whack, our cortisone levels are elevated significantly, our level of patience is little or none, and our agitation levels go through the roof. Our ability to be present goes out the window and we have little or no peace and so consequently as a result, our hormone levels are deflated which means that our sex lives and our ability to make love with our partner goes out the window as well. The same goes for a woman when her hormone levels are unbalanced—she's highly emotional. She can be very irrational, she can cry a lot. For a man, this is something he just doesn't know how to handle and so he has to leave and take a time-out.

In *Why Mars and Venus Collide*, John Gray talks about the "radically different responses to stress" which men and women typically exhibit: "Men tend to shift gears, disengage, and forget their problems, while women are compelled to connect, ask questions, and share problems. This simple distinction can be extremely destructive in a relationship if it is not appreciated and respected," he explains.

"When a man needs time alone or doesn't want to talk about his day, it doesn't mean that he cares less for his partner. When a women wants to talk about her day, it doesn't mean she is excessively needy or high-maintenance. His detached manner doesn't mean he doesn't care, and her stronger emotional reactions do not mean she doesn't appreciate all that he does to provide for her." In short, Dr. Gray asserts, "if a man forgets a woman's need or a woman remembers his mistakes, it doesn't mean they don't love each other."

He notes that in order for us to satisfy our partners' needs, we must to appreciate where they're coming from by developing an understanding of the inherent differences there are between us. If we can do that, ultimately we'll bring out the best in each other. "Instead of seeing our different stress reactions as a problem, we need to recognize that our attempts to change our partners are most often the real problem. Understanding the biological reasons for the different ways we perceive and behave in the world enables us to be realistic about what to expect from our partners," he writes.

Language, information, emotion, all these and more are processed quite differently by men and women. You see examples of that every day, Dr. Gray points out. "But now we have a way to make sense of this difference. Although happily married couples have already figured this out, finally the academic and scientific community has verified our different gender-related tendencies."

He cites the work of Harvard University sociobiologist Edward O. Wilson, who "has systematically observed our gender tendencies. He found that women are more empathetic and security-seeking than men and have more developed verbal and social skills. In comparison, men tend to be more independent, aggressive, and dominant and demonstrate greater spacial and mathematical skills."

If we fail to appreciate and allow for these contrasts, we are apt to view simple conflicts as much more complex and annoying than they really are. "For example," Dr. Gray offers, "when you discuss how you are going to invest your savings, a man is generally more of a risk taker and a woman will be more conservative. Certainly how we are raised will make a big difference, but generally speaking, men feel more comfortable taking risks, while women prioritize security. With an understanding of this difference, a man doesn't have to take it personally when she asks more questions. She is not necessarily mistrusting him but simply seeking to meet her greater need for security. When he is more impulsive and wants to find solutions right away, she can realize this is his nature rather than misinterpret his tone by presuming he doesn't care about what she feels, wants, or needs."

Research shows that men and women do not perceive such things as time, speed, mathematics, geographical orientation, and 3-D object visualization in the same way. "Men tend to excel in these skills," Dr. Gray asserts. "Women have more developed relationship abilities, sensitivity to emotions in others, emotional and aesthetic expression and appreciation, and language skills. Women are adept at performing detailed, planned tasks."

Consequently, a woman can tend to feel like her man is neglecting her when he doesn't immediately make time to be with her or doesn't allow for her needs. "If a woman understands these differences, she no longer resents needing to ask for support, because she realizes that his brain simply doesn't work the way hers does," he writes. "In the event that her partner does something without her having to ask, she will appreciate the extra effort he is making rather than taking it for granted.

"Women's brains are designed to consider and anticipate the emotions, sensitivities, and needs of others," he continues. "Men on the other hand, are more acutely aware of their own needs, or at least their needs for achieving the goal at hand. Since men were hunters for thousands of years, they needed this ability to protect themselves in the wild. In the home camp, a woman's life insurance was making sure she cared for others. If she did so, then they would care for her at her time of need."

Almost all women when they make out a will opt to designate their organs for donation after they die, he relates, while the exact reverse is true for men. "By nature, women tend to be giving, even after their death. A woman's greatest challenge in learning to cope more effectively with stress is to begin caring for herself as much as she is caring for others."

The problem is, the stimulation of hormone production tends to taper off when the first excitement of being in love subsides. At that point, "feel-good hormone levels begin to drop, and stress levels begin to rise. It is as if love gives us about three years of blissful hormones for free, but after the honeymoon period is over, we have to earn them," Dr. Gray suggests. "We have to manage our own stress levels as we interact with each other."

Let's pause here and draw a distinction between clinical stress and psychological stress. Unlike psychological stress, which is more of a state of mind based on such things as deadlines and irritating noises, clinical stress, the kind measured by scientists, Dr. Gray explains, is a physiological condition. Clinical stress refers to the production of certain hormones such as adrenaline or epinephrine and cortisol by the adrenal gland as a response to some exterior stimulation like a sudden fright or threat. The chemical reactions these hormones facilitate provide a heightened function of "the brain and muscles, sharpening our senses" increasing our physical strength and stamina and mental acuity. "This sudden focus redirects energy temporarily from other systems, slowing digestion and other secondary functions," he writes, enhancing your ability to confront or flee a perilous event. "For our ancient ancestors, these hormones were a survival mechanism in dangerous situations. Either we escaped or we were eaten."

Adrenaline and cortisol are useful in "life-and-death situations," but if they are often produced as a result of psychological stresses which are not life-threatening, it can be detrimental because "the body is not designed to accommodate the continual release of stress hormones," he points out. If this happens a lot, the ongoing presence of these hormones in our bodies can "disrupt our digestive and immune systems, resulting in lower energy and susceptibility to illness. With long-term stress, cortisol and adrenaline create unhealthy fluctuations in our blood sugar levels that can produce moodiness, mild depression, a sense of urgency, irritability, anxiety, and general distress. And all of these can affect our relationships."

Dr. Gray cautions that stress can adversely impact:

Our passion, through mild depression;

Our patience and flexibility, from an exaggerated sense of urgency;

Our ability to be happy, because of the sense of distress, anxiety, or panic it generates;

Our feelings of affection, appreciation, and tenderness, through heightened irritability;

Our generosity of spirit, from decreased energy levels;

Our moods, which can become deadened or fluctuate wildly because of changing blood sugar levels;

Men's engagement with their partner;

Women's sense of control and confidence in her ability to handle her responsibilities.

"When we understand the common symptoms of chronic stress," he says, "we can recognize why so many relationships fail today. Learning how stress affects our day-to-day behavior should motivate us to lower our own stress levels. By updating our relationship skills, we can convert our relationships to lower stress levels rather than being another source of stress."

Scientific research has shown a correlation between obesity caused by excessive fat storage and the hormone cortisol, he relates. "Stress and elevated cortisol levels tend to cause fat to deposit in the abdominal area, which is considered toxic fat, because it leads to strokes and heart attacks."

A tendency toward unhealthy eating can be caused by elevated levels of cortisol, research has shown. Studies indicate that "women with stress-induced high levels of cortisol were more likely to snack on high-fat or highly refined carbohydrate foods than women who did not secrete as much cortisol," Dr. Gray says. "This new research provides a useful insight into how stress can affect food cravings that lead to unhealthy eating. Have you ever noticed that when your are tired or stressed, you reach for some processed carbohydrate like cookies, chips, or soda?" he asks. "This is because under stress the body gets its energy from carbohydrates."

Heightened appetite is triggered by the cortisol because it is similar to the release of insulin. "This terrible cycle will cause you to gain weight and can eventually lead to diabetes and a host of other diseases," he warns. "The effects of high cortisol levels make it clear how important a healthy diet is when you are under stress. You might feel you do not have time to eat and prepare healthy meals, but maintaining good eating habits is even more important when you and your family are rushing through your lives. One of the ways you can know what foods are not good for you is simply observe what foods you crave when you are under stress. These are the very foods that will eventually make you feel even worse and put on extra weight. And let's face it, not only do we feel better when we are at a healthy weight, but we feel more attractive without the excess pounds. When you are feeling attractive, your partner becomes more attracted to you."

A woman's oxytocin levels can become depleted when her job involves testosterone-producing activities. Therefore, she can come to feel like her domestic duties and family and personal relationships can just be too much to deal with at the end of the day, according to Dr. Gray. That feeling of having so much to do and very little energy with which to do it can be highly stressful.

A man, on the other hand, views the end of the work day as the time to kick back and take it easy. "If he feels pressure to do more when he returns home, his tendency to relax is thwarted. With more responsibilities and less time to recover his testosterone levels, he has less and less energy. Instead of coming home to a sanctuary of love and support, both men and women today are confronted with new stress. Women need more of their partner's time and support, and men are running out of energy. Consequently, they both have less to give," he writes.

Often you'll hear a woman who is thinking about breaking up with her partner say things like, "I give and give, but I don't get back what I need. He just doesn't care, and I have nothing left to give," he relates.

"When a woman feels that her partner doesn't care about her needs, she becomes increasingly dissatisfied and resents that she is giving more than she is getting." The love may still be there, he says, but she is still ready to call it quits out of sheer exhaustion of being the only one who is putting anything into the relationship.

"Being in his presence no longer restores her oxytocin levels after a stressful day at work. Just anticipating being ignored or rejected by him can cause her oxytocin levels to drop and her stress levels to rise. Instead of being a source of support, her partner becomes another burden for her to carry," according to Dr. Gray. "If her partner understands her needs, it is a simple thing for him to give her a hug when they first meet after work and to spend a few minutes letting her talk about her day, both oxytocin boosters. Since she will be equally considerate of his needs, she won't be to demanding and will allow him to have the downtime he needs."

A woman wants to be successful in her job of course, but if that success not combined with balancing "her job-related testosterone-producing activities with oxytocin-producing activities and attitudes," her relationships will suffer. "Achieving success in a testosterone-producing activity can lower stress in men, but not in women. It is primarily the quality of her relationships that keeps a woman's stress levels down," he says.

When we looked in Chapter 5 at the time-out strategy for avoiding knock-down drag-out fights, we saw how our bodies naturally react to intense conflict with an urge go fight or flee. This "is an automatic full-body reaction to a perceived attack or threat to our survival that prepares us to defend ourselves," Dr. Gray explains. "The response is hardwired into our brains. When we are in danger, our brains activate the central nervous system." And as we've learned, hormones such as adrenaline and cortisol "are released into our bloodstreams, and our heart rate, blood pressure, and respiration are elevated. Blood is rerouted from our digestive tract and directed to our muscles and limbs to provide us with extra energy and fuel for running and fighting. Our awareness becomes more intense, our impulses faster. In this alert state, everything can be perceived as an enemy or threat to our survival. This physical response is a powerful emergency defense system in life-threatening situations."

The stress factors that we encounter in our everyday modern lives cause these hormones to be released. But because they are not actual physical threats that require us to respond with physical activity "we are not burning up or metabolizing the stress hormones." Threats that are only a matter of perception cannot be run from or physically fought. "Instead, we have to stay cool when we are criticized at the office, be patient spending hours on the phone with tech support trying to fix a computer glitch so we can meet a pressing deadline, sit in traffic without succumbing to road rage."

Our "fight or flight" response can become fully activated by many of the mental frustrations we encounter every day, causing "us to be aggressive or overreact. This physical response can have a devastating effect on our emotional and psychological states. We feel as if we are going from emergency to emergency. The buildup of stress hormones leads to physical ailments, including headaches, irritable bowel syndrome, hypertension, chronic fatigue, depression, and allergies."

In research conducted during his tenure at McGill University in Montreal, Hungarian-born stress expert Dr. Hans H.B. Selye "identified a three-stage response to this sort of stress on physiological, psychological, and behavioral levels," Dr. Gray relates. "Physically, our bodies go into the alarm stage, then the resistance stage, when our bodies begin to relax, and finally the exhaustion stage. Our psychological response to stress leads to feelings of anxiety, fear, anger, tension, frustration, hopelessness, and depression. On the behavioral level, we attempt to relieve the bad feelings that stress can cause. We eat too much or too little, drink or smoke too much, take more medications, or display fight-or-flight behavior by being argumentative or withdrawn respectively."

The hormone vasopressin is released when the fight-or-flight urge is induced in men, he notes. Testosterone enhances vasopressin, and when the two start working in combination oxytocin production becomes suppressed. The net effect then, is that men lack the natural tranquilizing effect of oxytocin that women have and thus have a much more difficult time getting themselves calmed back down after a stressful situation, he explains. "In day-to-day activities, women have much higher levels of emotional reaction, but at times of great danger, when men are ready to fight, it is often women who can calm things down."

One likely explanation for this evolutionary biological differ-ence, scientists think, is that ancient women needed to adapt their stress responses to compensate for times when they were "pregnant, nursing, or caring for children," Dr. Gray relates. "The 'tend-and-befriend' response involves tending to the young and befriending others in times of stress to increase the likelihood of survival. Since a group is more likely than an individual to overcome a threat, bond-ing is a protective mechanism for a mother and her children. While the men were out hunting, befriending other females was necessary for women's survival because pregnancy, nursing, and child care made women more vulnerable to outside threats."

This early form of "networking" was integral to women's safety and thus success in child-rearing. "Working in groups enabled them to gather food and tend to housing more effectively. In prehistoric times, males were drawn to larger groups to aid in defense and war, while females were drawn to smaller groups that provided emotional and caregiving support to other women during times of stress," he writes.

A fight-or-flight response would be of little use to women, who generally lacked the physical attributes of men and who, owing to their childbearing functions, from time to time would be in states of physical vulnerability, so they needed to find other ways of protect-ing themselves.

"This response to stress is still evident today in women's behav-ior. Rather than withdrawing or becoming belligerent, women seek social contact, especially with other women, and spend time nur-turing their children to cope with stress," We already have learned how "the production of oxytocin is directly linked to nurturing re-actions and behaviors. Situations and circumstances in which a woman is taking care of others or connecting emotionally are the most potent oxytocin stimulators," says Dr. Gray.

In their workaday worlds, women are forced to act according to financial demands or production goals and not according to the wellbeing of others and their behavior is constrained by the dictates of professional codes of conduct, thus constricting their production of oxytocin, he points out. "These are testosterone-producing situations. Though there is nothing wrong with stimulating testosterone, it does nothing to lower a woman's stress levels."

This can even be a problem for stay-at-home moms because although they enjoy the benefits deriving from the nurturing of child-rearing and housework, they are deprived of the natural support network perhaps their mothers enjoyed because many of their friends now work outside the home. "Some women even feel guilty or rejected by working women for choosing to stay at home rather than pursue a career. This sense of separation and abandonment only increases a woman's stress levels," he contends.

"Ultimately, women become stressed out when they do not take the time to do those things that will increase their oxytocin levels. To handle stress efficiently, a woman must integrate into her day a variety of oxytocin-producing experiences," Dr. Gray recommends. "She must cultivate a mindset and a support system of work, friends, and family who can stimulate the regular production of oxytocin. Without this support, she will expect too much of her partner. This insight releases a woman from depending too much on the man in her life to raise her oxytocin levels."

When a man gains insight into the types of activities that a woman needs to pursue to boost her oxytocin levels it will help him greatly toward learning why she does what she does. "For example," he reveals, "when a woman complains she is not getting enough support or feels the need to talk about the problems in her life, it does not mean she does not appreciate what her partner does. Instead, her behavior may be an indication that she is attempting to cope with stress by increasing her oxytocin levels." Thus, he writes, "Talking about problems with someone you love can elevate oxytocin levels on Venus."

Having that insight about a woman's motivations for conveying her thoughts on things that are important to her will put a man ahead of his brethren, most of whom are clueless when it comes to the stress-reducing effects of oxytocin. "Without understanding this biological drive, a man mistakenly assumes that a woman is looking for a solution from him. He interrupts her to give his solutions. He does so because solving problems is one of his ways to make himself feel better when he is stressed. He thinks it will help her, too. Solving problems raises his testosterone levels but does little for her oxytocin. Once a man understands that simply listening to his partner is enough to make her feel better, his testosterone levels go up as well, because he knows that he is actually solving a problem."

A further motivation for a man as well as a woman is that when she achieves the proper amount of oxytocin "the resulting lowered stress produces an endless source of energy as well as an ability to enjoy sex. Along with good communication, sexual intimacy can be one of the most powerful ways for a woman to lower her stress levels, because oxytocin is also produced by sexual arousal and orgasm."

It's sort of a Catch-22, though, he allows, because "most women first need oxytocin to feel sexual desire. Women who are very active sexually tend to want more sex, since sex produces a beneficial hormonal cascade. Women who have not had sex for a time often can do without it," he explains, "because they become too stressed. It's the use-it-or-lose-it response."

And that explains why making love is something most women don't even think of when they've finally made it through a long, high-pressure day. "It is often the last thing on their to-do list," he comments, adding that "most of the time stress inhibits a woman's desire for sex" as opposed to most men.

There are always exceptions, of course, and one such exception to this principle would be those women who have a stronger testosterone orientation and thus are not sex-inhibited by low oxytocin levels or stressful situations, Dr. Gray allows. "They are more like men, who can use sex to release their stress. When such a woman has sex, she finds some relief, but for different reasons than a man."

It is not long-lasting, but for these women, orgasm can cause oxytocin to become elevated and testosterone to be suppressed. "For a brief period, she is on vacation from her high testosterone levels. Sometimes high-testosterone women have a strong desire for sex but an inability to climax or an inability to be satisfied with one climax. Though this might sound exciting, it can be frustrating for both partners. A man wants to feel he can satisfy his partner, just as she wants to be satisfied. Oxytocin gives us the feeling of satisfaction. Too much testosterone can interfere with a woman's ability to have satisfying sex. Like eating a cookie laden with sugar, it tastes good but leaves her wanting more.

"Sexual activity produces testosterone in men," he continues, "but orgasm releases oxytocin. The calming effects of this hormonal cascade are why men often roll over and fall asleep afterward. After sex, a man's testosterone levels can drop for a while, which is why a man sometimes feels a need for greater distance immediately following sex."

The hormonal differences between men and women mean that their reactions to sexual activity can be very different, Dr. Gray declares. "While a woman's elevated oxytocin levels put her cuddle reflex in high drive, the dynamic of rising oxytocin and falling testosterone often causes a man to withdraw as his hormones return to their normal balance. Understanding and accepting that men sometimes retreat after sex, when women feel the most connected, can help avoid bad feelings."

One of the prime benefits of a lasting relationship can be rewarding sexual activity with your partner, he states. "To enjoy this gift for a lifetime, long after the newness wears off, men and women need to be creative in finding new ways to assist women in raising their oxytocin levels. When a woman is able to relax, she can once again enjoy her sexuality."

It would be a big mistake to think that our partner is hoping to get all the same things out of sex that we are. In fact, many times quite the opposite is true. Even though we share many of the same goals—such as a mutual desire "to be safe, happy, successful, and loved"—our means of achieving those goals "can be very different," according to Dr. Gray. "It is our hormones that make all the difference."

An article on the *Psychology Today* website on the same topic by San Francisco journalist Michael Castleman, a long-time author on sexuality, notes: "There are plausible biological reasons why, in general, men would want more sex than women. Male sex hormones (testosterone in men and a slightly different hormone in women) fuel libido in both genders, and men have much higher levels. Studies of transsexuals show that when men become women and take female sex hormones, they typically report mellowing of sexual desire, but when women become men and take testosterone, they usually say, 'As a woman, I liked sex but didn't feel driven to have it. Now I do.'"

Castleman agrees that the difference can be explained from an evolutionary standpoint. "The biological purpose of life is to reproduce life, to send one's genes into future generations. Women are most likely to do this by having a few children and nurturing them until they, too, reproduce. That works for men too, but men can also pursue another strategy—sex with as many women as possible to impregnate as many as possible."

Although these arguments carry much weight, they aren't always the case, Castleman says, noting, "if they truly explained desire differences between the genders, we would expect the overwhelming majority of men to want sex more often than the overwhelming majority of women. That does not appear to be the case."

A greater proportion of men do seem to desire sex more than women—as much as two-thirds according to many sex theapists, Castleman allows. "Now, this is a two-to-one margin, so partisans of the conventional wisdom can say, 'See? Men clearly want sex more than women.' All right. But if that's the case, why do somewhere around one-third of women want it more than men?" he muses.

One explanation, Castleman says, is offered in the book *Sex At Dawn: The Prehistoric Origins of Modern Sexuality*, by Christopher Ryan and Cacilda Jetha. The pair, Castleman relates, "marshall a great deal of psychological and anthropological research to support their view that if we remove the shackles of so-called civilization, women are just as libidinous as men and maybe more so. But for better or worse, we live in the world we inhabit, and the apparent enthusiastic promiscuity of prehistoric women doesn't alter our sexual norms today."

Should you find yourself in a relationship where the woman has the stronger sex drive, you can take comfort in knowing that it's not as strange as you've perhaps been led to believe by popular culture, Castleman points out. in one-third of couples who consult sex therapists, "Whatever the reason, if women want sex more , then after men say 'good-night,' the number of women who grit their teeth, or cry, or reach for the vibrator has to be in the millions."

So don't just dismiss your desire for more sex as "weirdness" and give up on seeking a change in your relationship, Castleman advises such women. Seek out a sex therapist who can help both of you come to terms with what actually is a much more normal condition than either of you probably think.

An understanding of the central thesis of Dr. Gray's book, "why Mars and Venus sometimes collide," can be attained by a familiarity with the hormonal differences in men's and women's stress coping mechanisms. "Social conditioning, parental example, and education can have a significant effect on how men and women interact and respond to each other, but how we react to stress is hardwired in our bodies and brains."

Little things can mean so much, but they can also drive us crazy, like socks on the floor, kids not cleaning up after themselves, nobody helping to wash the dishes, nobody helping to clean the table or help prepare the food. Women work so hard and as a result they have a built-in mechanism that allows them to work long hours. They also are vulnerable to stressing themselves out beyond their wildest imagination with not getting enough rest. This can be because when they go to bed they're not able to relax simply because they're overwhelmed with all the things they've had to do during the day.

Women like to do a lot of things, and that can lead to overdoing. Men, on the other hand, like to do one or two things, they like to stay focused on things and act as problem-solvers. Women like to prepare food, they're caretakers, that's their job. Men as I said earlier in this book, are providers and protectors. Their job is to protect the home, protect the children, protect their wives, and they do a good job of that. It's when they leave that they cause all the stress.

The goal of a successful relationship, Dr. Gray reminds us, is for both partners to live long, healthy lives so that they can grow old together. That can't happen if prolonged stress makes one or both become ill. "Heart disease, cancer, diabetes, and obesity have all been directly linked to chronically high levels of cortisol. If we learn to lower our stress levels, we will not only be healthier but will awaken our potential for increased energy, passion, patience, and happiness," he writes.

This is a particular risk for women because of the fact that stress results in higher levels of cortisone production in women than it does in men. "This helps explain why women have more challenges with weight gain," he relates. "When cortisol is elevated, we only burn carbohydrates or sugars for energy rather than a healthy combination of carbohydrate and fat. When you cannot burn fat efficiently, it is not only more difficult to lose weight, but you have less energy. Burning fat gives you twenty times more energy than burning carbohydrate. Think of it this way: burning fat gives us the lasting energy of burning logs, but carbohydrates only give us the quick, temporary energy of kindling," he explains.

"There is another costly effect of high cortisol levels on a woman's body. The by-product of burning carbohydrates is lactic acid. If a woman's body is burning carbohydrates instead of fat, her levels of lactic acid rise. With excess lactic acid buildup, calcium is leached from the bones to neutralize these acids. This helps explain why 80 percent of the people who have osteoporosis are women."

There also is a monetary cost of elevated cortisol levels owing to stress, he says, as it has been estimated that spending by both men and women on antidepressant drugs reaches into the billions of dollars annually. It doesn't have to be that way, as "there are natural ways to reduce stress levels that do not have the dangerous side effects of taking medications." Dr. Gray, whose research into the subject covers a decade, says that through such programs as "cleansing food plans, healthy fats, and natural supplements," men and women can deal with their stress and depression without such expensive, risky methods.

In my book, *Miracle Detox Secrets*, I discuss a variety of detoxification and cleansing methods that can help us relieve stress and achieve and maintain balance in our systems. It sounds like an unpleasant process, and most individuals I encounter cringe when I mention the word "detoxification." Images of a cold clinical probe invading their nether regions are enough to send them running in the other direction. Other avenues to detoxification can be just as discouraging because they require drinking a sludgy liquid that tastes like chalk or fasting for long periods of time. No wonder most people give up on the whole idea of cleansing.

Fortunately, though, there is a better way. My six-step detoxification plan is non-invasive, cost-efficient, extremely easy to implement, and delivers fantastic results.

Step 1: Select A Detoxification System

Look for a two-week to one-month detoxification program that uses only the finest ingredients available anywhere in the world. Check out my website, radiantgreens.com, for ideas. The program should stress weight loss, increased energy, and heightened mental clarity as well as promote a sensational feeling of overall well being. A key component should be a lineup of superior quality body cleansing nutrients, such as:

Aloe

Promotes healthy cleansing of deep tissues including the liver and kidneys,

Supports immune function,

Aids in effective digestion;

Herbal Teas

Stimulate entire digestive process, especially supporting stomach, liver, and the pancreas,

Act as mild diuretics by fostering the release of excess water;

Lipotropic Nutrients

Infuse the liver with the essential nutrients required for detoxification,

Increase the flow of bile, which escorts fat-soluble toxins from the liver,

Help to regulate fat metabolism;

Ionic Trace Minerals

Replenish the full spectrum of minerals that the body recognizes and quickly absorbs, but cannot manufacture on its own,

Regenerate the body's electrical system, boosting energy,

Release and expel harmful impurities that can cause a sluggish metabolism.

Such systems can help participants to rapidly drop an average of seven pounds by revving up their natural metabolic power to burn body fat for fuel instead of sending it to "storage" on your hips, thighs, or waistline. And they have the added benefit of scouring the body of toxic debris.

After trying a nine-day cleansing program for myself, I found that my bowel movements became more regular and substantial, providing me with a true feeling of detoxification. My girlfriend noticed almost immediately that I looked leaner and that my skin was positively glowing. After a few trips to the gym, I was thrilled when I was able to build my muscle mass more quickly than ever. At the same time, I felt a tremendous surge of energy and vitality.

Step 2: Eat a High-fiber Diet

A lot of people I meet with give me a blank stare when I ask if they get a lot of fiber in their diet. Even though fiber intake is an essential part of daily health and wellness, most folks fall short simply because they don't know which foods boost their fiber consumption. As it turns out, there is a wide array of foods that naturally contain fiber that are delicious and should be in your daily diet. These include:

Fruits: oranges, apples, pears, blackberries, strawberries, raspberries, and dried fruits such as apricots, prunes, and raisins;

Nuts and Seeds: almonds, flaxseed, and soy nuts;

Raw or Fresh Vegetables: broccoli, spinach, cabbage, green peas, kidney beans, and lima beans;

For a list of wheat-free, gluten-free products, see rad

Also, I have some suggestions for how you can boost your fiber levels with foods you may already be eating regularly:

Instead of a pepperoni pizza, get a "veggie delight" for an easy fiber "fix."

Choose brown rice over white rice. It's just as tasty but far more nutritious.

Have that morning bagel, but make it a whole grain one.

Find a 100 percent bran cereal you enjoy and cover it with fresh fruit.

Replace iceberg lettuce with a spinach salad instead.

Embellish as many meals as possible with vegetables and nuts.

Step 3: Drink More Water

My favorite fashion accessory in this country is the water bottle. Everyone seems to be carrying one, but are they drinking enough? I tell people to drink two 1.5-liter bottles (roughly equal to thirty-three ounces each) of water every single day.

When people don't drink enough water, dehydration can occur. Signs of dehydration aren't always obvious—bloating, headaches, dry-mouth, and a sluggish feeling are the most common.

Dehydration causes a "traffic jam" in the lymphatic system, which clogs the body's cleansing and filtration system. Constipation follows quickly on the heels of dehydration. Replenishing with water almost instantly clears the gridlock and gets your internal highway on the move again.

Step 4: Break a Sweat

The best stimulation for your body—including your colon—is exercise. Gentle aerobic exercise, such as brisk walking, gets your circulation going and works up a sweat. Because skin is the body's second largest organ of elimination, exercise is a great way to aid the detoxification process.

Exercise is a matter of personal preference. I always suggest that people experiment with different forms of exercise to see what they like best. Find something you love to do and you're more likely to meet the recommended goal of thrity minutes of exercise four to five times a week.

Some people thrive on going to the gym because they enjoy having access to all the expensive equipment, classes, and being exposed to social opportunities. Increased competition among fitness centers means joining a gym has never been easier or less expensive than it is today. Check out two or three local places to see where you are most comfortable and get started.

If gyms aren't your thing, you may find outdoor exercise very attractive because it offers visual stimulation as well as an opportunity to connect with nature and people. Walking, hiking, and biking are great ways to see and connect with the world while reaping the many rewards of exercising.

Longevity seekers know they can't spend their lives on the sofa with a remote in hand. But if you are short on motivation, remind yourself that even a moderate amount of exercise can substantially reduce your risk of death from heart disease and cancer.

Step 5: Skin Brushing

Another excellent way to help cleanse your body is with skin brushing. Skin brushing helps your skin eliminate waste acids and greatly assists the detoxification process. With the body making new skin every twenty-four hours, skin brushing keeps the uppermost layer free of dead cells that can impede oxygen absorption.

For optimal results, always use a natural bristle brush, never a nylon one, and never brush your face. In the shower, brush briskly upwards from toes to thighs, thighs to buttocks, finger tips to shoulders, pelvis to chest, and brush across your back. Brush vigorously enough to raise a pink glow on your skin.

With benefits that you can see and feel immediately, skin brushing gives your skin a satiny-smooth finish. There is now some evidence that it may break up cellulite too, so brush away!

Step 6: Make Favorite Food and Beverage Adjustments

I've learned the quickest way to make people tune out is to suggest they give up their daily double espresso, soda, or favorite snack. Instead, I recommend that people make substitutions or adjustments that don't leave them feeling depressed, angry, and resentful—which can lead to overindulging to compensate for feelings of deprivation.

Adjustments can be easy to implement. For example, if you rely on coffee or sodas for a "pick-me-up," try drinking a green tea beverage that gives you the same energy boost without all the toxic chemicals and sugar. Green tea is loaded with antioxidant-rich compounds and has been shown in research to help repress and prevent cellular changes that can lead to cancer.

When it comes to favorite food choices like ice cream or fettuccine Alfredo that thicken the waist line without any nutritional benefits, I say don't give them up entirely, just eat them less often. Try my "Five-Two Rule." In a nutshell, this is where you aim for consuming the health-enhancing foods and beverages I mentioned above five days a week. For the remaining two days, give yourself leeway to revisit some favorite indulgences, whether it's a 650-calorie coffee drink or a chocolate chip cookie.

Most people who try my Five-Two Rule actually begin to notice a big difference in how they feel when they slowly but surely say goodbye to bad food habits without any regrets whatsoever. Some even find themselves extending it to a seven-day routine because they find they don't really miss the high-calorie foods they previously thought they had to have. For more information, read *Miracle Detox Secrets* or visit radiantgreens.com.

In this chapter we've learned how the stress we may be feeling personally can cause stress in our relationships with others. And in our modern day world, often with both partners working, that stress can become extreme and cause our hormones to become unbalanced. We've seen how stress can affect men and women differently. Men and women have developed different mechanisms for coping with stress, and we've learned that there can be adverse consequences for assuming that we react in the same way. It's been enlightening to learn how evolutionary demands have played a strong role in creating the difference in how males and females are affected by and react to stress.

We've also seen that stress-related fluctuations in hormonal levels can play a critical role in both our mental outlook and our physical wellbeing and how crucial it is that we understand these effects in both ourselves and our partners. Such an appreciation empowers us to be more sensitive to our partner's needs. Sometimes a small act—like a well-timed hug or lending a sympathetic ear—can make a huge impact. When we learn that we've been conditioned by society to view some of our behaviors as "weird"—such as a woman wanting sex more often than a man—and that such conditioning is not borne out by natural facts, it helps us realize that conflicts arising out of these differences can be resolved or at least alleviated through understanding and counseling.

Finally, this chapter has shown us the helpful role cleansing can play in getting our hormones back in balance and our stress under control. Biologically, we are stressed more than ever before. We need to effect change by simply resting. Getting more rest is one of the keys to offsetting hormonal imbalance, and when we do so, then we can have a much more joyous life and that's what we're all seeking.

In the next chapter, we'll deal with those times in a relationship when understanding breaks down and the man or the woman or both start to entertain thoughts of looking for a new partner.

CHAPTER 8

AFFAIRS: DON'T LET THEM CAUSE A BREAKUP

When you are stressed, it puts pressure on a relationship and that pressure often manifests itself in fights and arguments, as we saw in the previous chapter. The alienation and dissatisfaction that results can also cause one or both partners to start looking outside the relationship for companionship. When that happens, the results can be devastating and, ultimately, may lead to a breakup.

In relationships where both partners are working and they have a nanny doing the duty at home, making dinners, taking care of the kids, and so on and so forth, it's very hard to have a love life and to have a connection. It winds up being a situation where there's competition within the workplace and also within the home for who brings in the most amount of money. There's a power struggle, there's an ego struggle, and this can lead to or amplify differences of opinion that are already present.

These days, it seems like as many women are having affairs in the workplace as men. It's unfortunate, but this is what happens, and this is what drives a wedge between a man and a woman—our differences and our lack of respect and honor for each other. We feel like we are not being heard and we're not being understood in our relationship. Meanwhile, somebody else, perhaps a co-worker, is hearing you and understanding what you're saying and if it's a male colleague, then the woman can be attracted to him and if it's a female co-worker then the man can become attracted by what he hears her saying to him. Either way, the person is getting input and feedback from an interesting someone of the opposite sex that they aren't getting from their significant other at present. Feelings of guilt can become mixed with a sensation of excitement and curiosity and consequently as a result, you can find yourself entering into a relationship and perhaps even having an affair. This may cause such division within the relationship that it could culminate in a separation or divorce.

It's a huge issue that goes on simply because we sometimes just don't respect each other enough or we don't listen to each other and we feel terribly misunderstood. The importance a husband showing respect for his wife can't be overstated, and forms one of the central tenets of Emerson Eggerichs' book, Love & Respect. "Over the years," he relates, "many men have come to me and said,

> 'You know, pastor, my prayer life isn't what it should be.'
> I respond, 'How are you treating your wife?'
> 'No, no,' the husband hastens to explain, 'my prayer life isn't where it ought to be.'
> 'How are you treating your wife?'
> 'No, no, pastor, I'm saying my prayer life, I'm not talking about my wife.'
> I smile and say, 'I'm talking about your wife.' "

There are scriptural reasons that husbands should honor their wives as equals, Dr. Eggerichs points out, noting that I Peter 3:7 tells husbands to live in an understanding way with their wives and to show them honor. "Tucked into I Peter 3:7 is one more phrase that every husband should heed: Peter adds that the reason the husband should treat his wife in an understanding way . . . is so that his prayers will not be hindered. That is why I would often tell men who came to see me for counsel that if Heaven seems silent to their prayers, perhaps they were not honoring their wives as God intended. These men were sure they were doing all the right things—walking in integrity and serving the Lord—but when they prayed, the heavens seemed as brass. They kept wondering, 'God, why aren't you hearing me?' And as we probed a little deeper we often saw that the answer with these men was that they weren't living with their wives in an understanding way that honored and esteemed them. As soon as these men started obeying scripture, their prayer life improved."

Dr. Eggerichs frames this portion of his book around the acronym, "C.O.U.P.L.E.," which, he explains, "is a commentary on the best way to show respect to a wife. The best way to respect or honor a wife is through your closeness, openness, understanding, peacemaking, loyalty, and . . . esteem. A wife who is esteemed will not sing Aretha Franklin's refrain, 'R-E-S-P-E-C-T.' Scripture speaks of how a man should esteem and cherish his beloved. The Song of Solomon 7:6 says: 'How beautiful and how delightful you are, my love, with all your charms.' A husband is to be one who cherishes his wife (Ephesians 5:29). The well-known passages of Proverbs 31, 28 and 29, say, 'Her children stand up and call her blessed. Her husband also rises up and he praises her. He says, 'Many women do noble things, but you are better than all the others.' "

Asserting that "God has made women so that they want to be esteemed and respected," he continues, "The way to honor your wife, as well as to honor your covenant with God, is to treasure her. When I say your wife wants honor and respect, it is a different kind of honor from what you seek as a man. For her, respect is a part of love. Probably the only time when you'll hear her say, 'You don't respect me,' is when you dismiss her opinion. Actually her exact words might be: 'I know you don't love me because you don't respect me

You wife wants to know that you have her on your heart and mind first and foremost. This is what I mean by esteem. When it's there, your wife will feel treasured as if she's the most loved woman on earth. Also, she will want to respect you in a similar way that the church reverences Christ. Remember that your love motivates her respect and her respect motivates your love."

So what we say to each other should matter but for some people and for some couples, what he says doesn't matter and what she says doesn't matter and as a consequence, we get tired and we get bored of each other and as a result, people just say, 'I've had enough.' Under these circumstances, somebody else comes along that's far more exciting than your husband or some other woman comes along that's far more exciting to the man. The new man lights her fire and the new woman lights his fire and as a result, the original couple ends up separating.

The sad thing is that generally these types of encounters are short-lived—they're just creatures of the momentary dissatisfaction that one or both partner is experiencing in their relationship and usually don't last. So then what's left is a whole lot of regret and remorse. It could have all been avoided if the couple had just sat down, paused in their conflicts, and perhaps sought some professional outside help. This is why therapy can be very important for everybody.

In *What You Feel You Can Heal*, John Gray comments: "Let's take a closer look at the 50 percent of relationships that 'succeed.' Stop right now and ask yourself this question: 'How many couples do I know whom I admire, whose relationship seems like one I would like to have for myself?' If you are like most people, you will have a hard time coming up with many examples of 'good relationships.' Between 40 and 70 percent of married couples aren't satisfied with their partners and have had outside affairs. One recent survey showed that the greater the household income, the more affairs the couples had. It's obvious from these statistics that money is not the solution to marital happiness. The American dream of a house, two cars, and a happy family has ended in divorce all too many times."

It is often the case that instead of meeting the hangups in a relationship head-on, acknowledging the dissatisfactions that exist, people will simply ignore the difficulties and muddle on. These people, Dr. Gray suggests, "pretend to be happy when they are really feeling resentful, sad, or numb. They must pretend because if would hurt too much to look at the truth. They are afraid to look at their problems because they don't have a solution. So they keep up the appearance of a relationship while all the time they are dying inside. Sometimes the loneliest place in the world is lying next to someone who doesn't love you anymore or someone you have stopped loving. How many times have you felt surprised when you heard friends of yours were getting a divorce or splitting up? On the surface everything looked great, but the love was dead."

Oftentimes people are at a loss to know what to do about the troubles in their marriage or relationship and so cast around for some method of dealing with them, Dr. Gray notes. "The first option, of course, is to just ignore the problems and hope that they will go away. Another method is to justify the problem and tell yourself that there is no such thing as the 'perfect' relationship, and to expect more is immature and unrealistic. You can also try blaming it all on your partner. You may even leave that partner and find another, only to find yourself facing the same problems all over again. Some people go from partner to partner, trying to avoid conflict and problems. And others decide that it is less scary to stay stuck in a relationship than to risk leaving it, and they just give up."

Dealing with an affair is very difficult, very sensitive, and can be devastating for either party if it isn't handled with care and consideration. Relationships can survive them, but it takes an awful long time and it definitely needs therapy. It's something that you shouldn't try to work out on your own at home because there's too much judgment passed and there's a tremendous amount of resistance and resentment as a result.

What drives people to affairs in the first place is attraction—physical attraction. These are people that are drawn to each other but who will never marry each other. Often with men there's a sexual component of the physicality of another woman. If things are going really, really great in the home, things at home are magnificent, it's a two-way street. Men don't want to have affairs and women don't want to have affairs. But if things are not going great in the home, if you're not treating each other with honor and respect and there's no integrity and you're not being sensitive to each other's needs and desires and feelings and you're not making love on a consistent basis, generally people start to look outside their relationship, looking for an affair.

We have to work at relationships because they're difficult, they're challenging, they're stressful. It's very different now from how it was for my parents and your parents—very different from forty to fifty years ago when things were slow and easygoing, and the divorce rate was not high. People generally didn't get divorced, they worked through their differences. If they didn't work through their differences they still lived together. They would never think of having a separation.

If an affair takes place, often that can be the end of a relationship but not always. If there's enough love in the relationship it can be held together provided of course that one goes to therapy. This is why I highly recommend that couples seek therapy as much as possible. Even when things are good they should seek therapy because drama and emotional issues can come up and when they do come up you need to know how to deal with them. You have to be a great coach. You need to know what to say, what not to say, when to speak, when not to speak, and when to listen. You should always listen. And you need to know how to really connect in a way that shows your partner that you trust them, you love them, you care for them, and that you'd never do anything to hurt them.

But in the case of an affair. You have to really fight back and find a way to prove your love to this person. Because if you've done it once they're thinking in the back of their mind, 'Well, maybe he'll do it a second time and a third time', and then that's the end of the relationship. Many women unfortunately stay in relationships when their partners cheat on them and many men stay in relationships when women cheat on them simply because they have children together and they do it for the sake of the children. Once the children are grown up and they've gone off to school or they've gone off to do their own thing, then the couple separates. So they wait for ten or twelve years and they live in a loveless marriage.

That's probably not the way to go. Yes, for the sake of the children it's a wonderful thing, but for the sake of the two people, they're generally living in misery. So this is why I encourage people to seek therapy. It's really that important to understand their differences, why this happened, and how they can come back together again and maybe stronger than ever before. Once therapy is in place, then they can really understand why their difficulties happened in the first place. It's important that one of the parties seeks forgiveness because if you don't seek forgiveness you can't build the trust and if you can't build the trust then there's no honor or respect and then there's no relationship—there's no opportunity for you to really build a relationship again moving forward.

And a lot of times this is how affairs start because if hormone levels are deflated men and women, both at the same time, can become bored with each other. Both are irritated at each other, both are highly agitated, both are fighting all the time, there's a tremendous amount of stress and conflict going on, everything she does drives him crazy and everything he does drives her crazy and as a result, there's no connection, there's no level of intimacy and there's no lovemaking and as a result, one or the other of the partners will tend to seek a relationship with someone who makes them feel good, who raises their hormone levels and raises their testosterone levels.

This is a huge issue in our country simply because of the high stress levels and because of the high workload and because of two people working outside of the home. So if you've got high stress levels you've got a lot of agitation and because you've got a lot of agitation you have little or no connection and hormone levels are at an all-time low. There are people who are very stressed, many others suffer from adrenal exhaustion, while others suffer from chronic fatigue, and life won't be very exciting, certainly not in the bedroom. Everyone around me here in L.A. has been divorced, primarily as a result of alcohol abuse, which is a huge issue. And the root cause of the substance abuse is issues at home.

Women drink just as much as men. Women are having more affairs now, according to research, than men. So the gender role has shifted significantly, and this trend has even meant that a lot of women become lesbians because there's no connection in their heterosexual relationship and when there's no connection, then they go seek other relationships whether it's gay, lesbian, whatever. It becomes a huge issue.

One study indicating that women are engaging in affairs in increasing numbers was cited by writer Jay Dixit in his article, "Sex Ed: The Cheat Sheet," posted on the *Psychology Today* website. "In a classic experiment," he writes, "researchers asked men and women in committed, monogamous relationships how likely they'd be to cheat on their significant others. Men reported being much more willing to cheat. But when they were later offered the chance to go on a date with a stranger, the gender gap closed. Women in relationships were just as likely as men to seize the opportunity."

Dixit reports that studies by University of Southern California at Los Angeles psychologist Martie Haselton and anthropologist Elizabeth Pillsworth has found that "women are most likely to cheat when they're ovulating." Calling this period a "fertile window," they note that women experiencing ovulation "become more attracted to masculine men—muscular, symmetrical, socially dominant guys with pronounced brows and strong jawlines—providing their current mates don't already have those characteristics. Women pursue a 'dual mating strategy,' says Pillsworth, settling down with a partner who'll invest resources in her and her children but seeking out prime genes by having sex outside the relationship. Tall women also cheat more—possibly because testosterone may influence height and infidelity."

Another key factor is the personality of the man or woman involved, Dixit notes. "Men with high self-esteem cheat more, maybe because they think they're entitled. Wealth magnifies the effect. Women with low self-esteem are more unfaithful, maybe because they're seeking affirmation outside the relationship."

Physical appearance plays a role too, adds University of Minnesota researcher Kristina Durante, who asserts that "the real culprit is the hormone estradiol, an indicator of fertility," Dixit writes. "Fertile women tend to be very attractive, and estrogen tells their brains they have options."

Finally, a person's perception of what is and is not accepted or usual behavior in a given environment can also affect whether they'll have an affair. "Encouraging women to think they have options—say by reading a fake news story announcing a surplus of single men in town—makes them less satisfied with their partners, which in turn leads to cheating. The same holds for men. As comedian Chris Rock put it, 'You're only as faithful as your options.'" Dixit writes.

Funny, yes, but that's a pretty cynical view of things. It doesn't have to be that way if a couple makes consideration of each other a central part of their relationship. John Gottman points out that there is a solid body of evidence to suggest that one of the key ingredients of a successful relationship is whether a spouse returns the kindnesses he or she receives from their partner. "In other words," he writes in *Seven Principles For Making Marriage Work*, "they meet a smile with a smile, a kiss with a kiss. When one helps the other with a chore, the other intentionally reciprocates, and so on. In essence, the couple function with an unwritten agreement to offer recompense for each kind word or deed. In bad marriages this contract has broken down; so that anger and resentment fill the air. By making the floundering couple aware of the need for some such 'contract,' the theory goes, their interactions could be repaired."

In a failing relationship this sort of "quid pro quo" takes an ugly turn, with the aggrieved spouse keeping close track of each nice thing they've done and noting every time it wasn't returned by their partner. "Happy spouses do not keep tabs on whether their mate is washing the dishes as a payback because they cooked dinner. They just do it because they generally feel positive about their spouse and their relationship. If you find yourself keeping score about some issue with your spouse, that suggests it's an area of tension to your marriage."

It's simply a myth that "avoiding conflict will ruin your marriage," Dr. Gottman says. " 'Tell it like it is' has become a pervasive attitude," he writes, "but honesty is not best for all marriages. Plenty of lifelong relationships happily survive even though the couple tend to shove things under the rug." One couple he has counseled has found that they can best deal with their arguments through a system of mutual avoidance, he relates. The husband switches on a sports channel on the television when he becomes upset with his wife, while her strategy is to go shopping. "Then they regroup and go on as if nothing happened. Never in forty years of marriage have they sat down to have a 'dialogue' about their relationship. Neither of them could tell you what a 'validating' statement is. Yet they will tell you honestly that they are both very satisfied with their marriage and that they love each other deeply, hold the same values, love to fish and travel together, and wish for their children as happy a married life as they have shared."

The best way for couples to deal with their problems is with whatever works for them, he allows. "Some avoid fights at all costs, some fight a lot, and some are able to 'talk out' their differences and find a compromise without ever raising their voices. No one style is necessarily better than the other—as long as the style works for both people. Couples can run into trouble if one partner always wants to talk out a conflict while the other just wants to watch the playoffs."

And when that trouble starts getting out of hand, it can often lead ultimately to a split. The toxic atmosphere that is created in the relationship as these troubles and misunderstandings worsen can create a situation ripe for one or both partner to have an affair. If a total breakup does finally occur though, more times than not, it is the relationship problems that lie at the center of the cause, not the affair itself.

"Problems in the marriage that send the couple on a trajectory to divorce," agrees Dr. Gray, "also send one (or both) of them looking for intimate connection outside the marriage. Most marital therapists who write about extramarital affairs find that these trysts are usually not about sex but about seeking friendship, support, understanding, respect, attention, caring, and concern—the kind of things that marriage is supposed to offer."

A key finding of "probably the most reliable survey ever done on divorce"—a study in Corte Madera, California by the Divorce Mediation Project's Lynn Gigy, Ph.D., and Joan Kelly, Ph.D.—was that "80 percent of divorced men and women said their marriage broke up because they gradually grew apart and lost a sense of closeness, or because they did not feel loved and appreciated," he reports. "Only 20 to 27 percent of couples said an extramarital affair was even partially to blame."

Despite what many people would perhaps like to believe, affairs don't "just happen," according to relationships expert Michele Weiner-Davis, director of The Divorce Busting Center in Boulder, Colorado. "Affairs aren't spontaneous; they require careful planning and decision-making," she writes in the article, "I Wasn't Looking for an Affair, It Just Happened," posted on the *Psychology Today* website. "Often, the choices people make that pave the way for an affair—dinner with a co-worker, meeting an old boyfriend or girl-friend for a drink after work just to catch up, having lunch with an attractive, single neighbor on a regular basis or sending a lengthy Christmas update to a long lost heartthrob—can seem relatively in-nocent," says the founder of divorcebusting.com.

People who make such arrangements are asking for trouble at best and fooling themselves at worst, she says, because "one dinner date or late night conversation often leads to another and another and another. The talk becomes more personal. Confessions of mar-ital dissatisfaction bubble to the surface prompting empathy and support. People tell themselves, 'I just needed someone to talk to. I wanted input from someone of the opposite sex.' But you don't need a degree in psychology to know that the implicit message in these conversations is, 'I'm unhappily married. Want to fool around?' You can tell yourself that you're not doing anything wrong, but the truth is it's a sheer, slippery slope."

Add alcohol to the mix, Weiner-Davis comments, and it's a ver-itable sure-fire recipe for extra-marital hanky-panky, and a situa-tion you've entered into with eyes wide shut. Even though "it's true that many a bad decision has been made while under the influence, unless like teenagers in Cancun on spring break, people's mouths are forced open and alcohol poured down their throats, having a drink is a decision. Having two drinks is two decisions. You can do the math on the rest of the story."

The complaint of a bad marriage is hardly a valid excuse for an affair, she maintains, because there's no direct correlation of one with the other. "What's always amazed me is how differently people react to similar circumstances. I've met people whose spouses re-fused to have sex for years and although that made them miserable, they simply could not cheat. I've met other people who, when their relationships hit predictable bumps in the road, rather than work things out, they sought comfort in the arms of strangers. Unhappy marriages don't cause infidelity. Being unfaithful causes infidelity."

She concedes that "life is short and feeling lonely in marriage is not the way to live. But dulling one's pain through the instant gratification of hot sex or emotional closeness with someone who doesn't argue with you about bills, children, or the in-laws isn't an effective or lasting way to fix what's wrong. In fact, infidelity complicates life enormously for everyone involved, a fact that should not be minimized when planning the next 'just friends' at Starbucks break."

It could be, Weiner-Davis allows, that "people who say their affairs 'just happened' aren't necessarily intentionally trying to cover their asses or justify their behavior; they often truly believe what they're saying. They simply lack insight or awareness of the ways in which their actions, however subtle, have created their current predicaments. But in the same way that affairs don't just happen, neither does healing from betrayal. Unless those who have strayed look inward and take personal responsibility for the paths their lives have taken, they will not be able to get back on track when they've gotten derailed. In my view, being unconscious just doesn't cut it."

That's certainly how I see things as well. Like I said earlier in this book, it's vital for the health of your relationship to be mindful rather than mindless. Don't let disagreements or problems you may be having become an excuse for straying into an affair that you'll come to regret and which could end up destroying your marriage or relationship. It's traumatic enough for you and your partner, but if there are children involved, it's doubly bad. In the next chapter, we'll take a look at the family dynamic in relationships.

And if one of you does stray, however, don't just automatically think all is lost. As we've seen, an affair, though devastating, doesn't necessarily have to be the end. Even though times have changed and more women are having affairs and divorce is more common and socially acceptable, you don't have to be one of those statistics. Through patience and forgiveness, you can survive this.

CHAPTER 9

WHEN KIDS ENTER
THE RELATIONSHIP

T he dynamic of children can have a ground-shifting impact on a relationship. In *Seven Principles* John Gottman writes, "Virtually every study that has looked at how people make the transition from couplehood to parenthood confirms" the view that "a baby sets off seismic changes in a marriage. Unfortunately, most of the time those changes are for the worse. In the year after the first baby arrives, 70 percent of wives experience a precipitous plummet in their marital satisfaction. For the husband, the dissatisfaction usually kicks in later, as a reaction to his wife's unhappiness. There are wide-ranging reasons for this deep disgruntlement—lack of sleep, feeling overwhelmed and unappreciated, the awesome responsibility of caring for such a helpless little creature, juggling mothering with a job, economic stress, and lack of time to oneself, among other things."

Indeed, the reasons for dissatisfaction are so obvious and numerous, it's actually more surprising that so many women—in the neighborhood of 30 percent, according to his research—have no difficulty making the adjustment whatsoever. "In fact," comments Dr. Gottman, "some of these mothers say their marriage has never been better. Thanks to the 130 couples we've followed from their newlywed stage to as long as eight years afterward, I now know the secret to keeping a marriage happy and stable even after the 'grenade' explodes. What separates these blissful mothers from the rest has nothing to do with whether their baby is colicky or a good sleeper, whether they are nursing or bottle-feeding, working or staying home. Rather, it has everything to do with whether the husband experiences the transformation to parenthood along with his wife or gets left behind."

When a woman becomes a mother, it is virtually guaranteed that she will experience a profound psychological and physical change in her life. "She has never felt a love as deep and selfless as the one she feels for her child," Dr. Gottman declares. "Almost always a new mother experiences nothing less than a profound reorientation of meaning in her life. She discovers she is willing to make enormous sacrifices for her child. She feels awe and wonder at the intensity of her feelings for this fragile little being."

Naturally, given how profound the change is for the woman, there can be a tension between her and her husband if he doesn't share her new attachment equally. "While the wife is embracing a new sense of 'we-ness' that includes their child," Dr. Gottman explains, "the husband may still be pining for the old 'us.' So he can't help but resent how little time she seems to have for him now, how tired she always is, how often she's preoccupied with feeding the baby. He resents that they can't ride bikes to the beach anymore because the baby is too small to sit up in a back carrier. He loves his child, but he wants his wife back."

When tensions between partners are present in families with older children, the responses of those children can further complicate matters. The impact on a relationship from the "See-Saw Effect" which John Gray discusses in *What You Feel, You Can Heal* and which we were introduced to back in Chapter 2, can take on dramatic proportions when older children are added to the mix. When kids are present, the principle becomes "What you suppress, your children express."

The thinking of a lot of couples seems to be that it's important to try to shield their kids from emotional trauma by concealing their emotions. "I feel this couldn't be further from the truth," Dr. Gray declares. The primary reason for that is that it simply is not possible. "Your children will pick up on your feelings anyway, whether you choose to express them consciously or not, and the kids will only feel confused by the mixed messages and may even start feeling that they are responsible for making you unhappy."

Kids naturally sense it when angry tension exists between their parents, and if you try to keep it from them, you can expect them to "act out through angry, rebellious behavior and temper tantrums," Dr. Gray maintains. "If a parent is suppressing his sadness and hurt, the children will cry more. If a parent is pushing down his feelings of fear and insecurity, the children may whine and become more fearful."

It's a real dilemma, but Dr. Gottman suggests that the solution may actually be relatively simple: the husband must just face the reality of the situation and accept that he can't have his old wife back because she's gone forever. Instead he needs to fully embrace this new wife who, after all, is basically the same person only with new responsibilities and priorities. "Only then can their marriage continue to grow. In marriages where the husband is able to do this, he doesn't resent his child. He no longer feels like only a husband, but like a father, too. He feels pride, tenderness, and protectiveness toward his offspring."

All parties need to be heard in a relationship, including the children. A good time for that to happen is during regular family gatherings. Dinnertime is an excellent time when you have younger children because it takes place every single night. Eating and having meals is a beautiful way to celebrate your children, to celebrate life, and to celebrate the joys and the blessings that you have and, again, to connect and to communicate in a joyous, harmonious way.

If the children are a little older, you can plan family get-togethers once or twice a week. It's also very important to schedule a family night once or twice a week. Once a week is definitely a good starting point to allow the children to be heard because it's very important that you hear what they have to say as well. They need to be understood. There are always going to be misunderstandings, there are always going to be demands on your partner's time, your time, and your children's time, plus there are differing sets of desires and needs that must be taken into account. Therefore, it is essential that you all communicate frequently and effectively in order to minimize the friction among you.

When it's back to school time, for instance, kids want to get clothes ready, as you can imagine, they want to make sure that they have everything that they need to go back to school. Parents are being pulled in many different directions—they're working fifteen, sixteen hours a day, and this is pretty much seven days a week, they're preparing dinner, they're transporting the kids all over, going to soccer practice, going to basketball practice, going to swimming classes, going to football practice, they're going to so many things. But still, parents need to make time for communication. Children need to hear what their parents have to say and parents need to hear what their children have to say so they're all on the same page and so there's more connection.

In an article posted on the *Psychology Today* website, psychologist Abigail Brenner recommends establishing "family traditions" as a means of bringing everyone closer together. These traditions can be developed on a daily basis and may be scheduled for varioius times of the year as well, she offers in "5 Ways to Create Family Traditions and 5 Reasons Why We Should." The traditions she has in mind "are those special times that bring families together, allowing us to express unity as a family and to create bonds that last a lifetime. Since every family unit is unique unto itself, the traditions created by each family are sure to be unique and special to the whole family unit as well as to each of its members individually."

Such routine activities as bedtime preparations or "talking, reading, snuggling up together, and saying a prayer" can be important points of connection throughout the day. "Spending time alone with each child," she suggests, "such as having dinner with individual children or doing a hobby or project together, personalizes experiences and affords parents the opportunity to recognize and encourage each child's special qualities. Weekly family meetings (perhaps with a favorite dinner) allows for discussion of upcoming schedules and activities for each family member and provides a forum to air differences, raise important issues, and plan ahead for the family," she writes.

Annual family events can also be fun to establish and can be something family members look forward to all year. One idea she offers is to celebrate spring with "camping, hiking, or going fishing." Another "event anticipated weeks ahead of time" can be the first ballgame, while "a picnic to a favorite place or a backyard BBQ for friends and neighbors can create an atmosphere of cooperation in the planning and preparation for the event." Another useful activity would be a "spring cleaning day around the house," Dr. Brenner suggests, "or perhaps a day annually or monthly to lend a hand within the community."

Planning occasions which pay tribute to family history is another great way to bind families together, she writes. "These traditions provide a sense of continuity and cultural identity and allow us to explore the similarities, the things that resonate within each of us individually, with our ancestors. Visiting the cemetery to the gravesites of family members is common to many cultures and affords the family a time to honor and remember those who have gone before us."

Another way to celebrate your family's culture would be to visit your ancestral homeland, Dr. Brenner says. "Beyond hearing stories about one's ancestors, making a trip of 'discovery' to the mother country, the home of one's ancestors, puts families up close and personal with the land and landmarks of one's relatives." Another idea is to incorporate "Bibles, wine cups, candlesticks, baptismal outfits, Christmas ornaments, etc." into special family occasions. "Birthdays, anniversaries, and other personal family events are occasions to establish any number of traditions, such as a favorite cake or meal, or visiting a place closely associated with the event," she says.

Associations with compatible religious or ethnic groups or those who "share ideas and beliefs" can be recognized as well, Dr. Brenner suggests. "Beyond what we have in common, though, families can learn together about other spiritual traditions by visiting local houses of worship and participating in holidays and celebrations of other traditions. This practice encourages tolerance, acceptance, and diversity."

Such occasions can become more than just a means of bringing everyone together, she says. "Traditions establish and strengthen family bonds by providing a solid structure, a sense of continuity, and a feeling of belonging. Family teaches values. Traditions support and communicate a family's belief system. They instill faith and convey the family's perspective on life experiences. The immediate family serves as your witnesses through life's transitions, sharing and committing to each other in times of joy and celebrations, and lending support and comfort through crises, disappointments, and losses. Family traditions are part of the 'language' of a family, a shorthand, symbolic way of relating that everyone understands. As life moves forward and people grow and change, family traditions keep us connected. For sure, they create memories for everyone to share for a lifetime, and even beyond."

I think exercise provides an excellent opportunity for family connection. Everyone needs exercise, but it can be time consuming, so a great way to get exercise and have family time simultaneously is through sports. Families should play sports together, they should swim together, they should exercise together, they should go shopping together if at all possible. Any form of connection is good. Any form of sports is good. Volleyball, basketball, table tennis. I play table tennis with my family, I exercise with my family, I hike with my family, I run with my family, I workout with my family, I do all those types of exercises so that we have a better connection.

Vacations are another great opportunity for togetherness. In my family, we go in our RV for trips up the coastline, down the coast, we do all those things that families like to do. These things are very important because if you do these things you have a better connection with your family, the kids are happier, they're more connected, they're free of conflict when they're playing, and they're joyous. Vacations for children are always wonderful, although vacations can become exceptionally expensive. Likewise, school time is exceptionally expensive now for kids, especially if they go to college. Books and tuition and so on and so forth. Definitely vacations are important. These are bonding times with your kids and every child I know looks forward to a vacation, so plan as many vacations as you can within your financial resources. If at all possible, go away for at least ten days. Two weeks is always a good amount of time for taking a break, not only for the parents but also for the children as well. Just have a magnificent time, whether it's overseas if it can be afforded, or across this great country which we call America. There are lots of beautiful sights to be seen and lots of opportunities to explore, so swim and enjoy the ocean, and connect with other couples on the beach and really start to live and enjoy.

Dr. Brenner recommends giving "each family member . . . an opportunity to weigh in on choosing where the family should go. Family trips," she adds, "can also have themes, such as ecology, learning about the environment, working on a farm or ranch, or 'service trips' such as helping a community at home or abroad." They can also "include traveling to reunions to visit with extended family. An annual vacation may be purely for rest, relaxation, and fun, or may have an educational bent, such as a visit to a cultural/historical site or one that reflects a specific place or event that is being studied in school."

We need more connection in our lives. What happens a lot of the time unfortunately in Los Angeles is that many kids are raised by their nanny which is O.K., but their real parents never get a chance to really get to know their kids until they're too old or if the kids get into trouble. That's unfortunately something that can result when there's little or no connection.

Many kids have low levels of self-esteem. There's a lot of peer pressure on kids to excel, to exceed, and to do well in school, to get the right grades and be academically brilliant. There's a lot of pressure on kids to do well, particularly if they come from well-to-do families. The father has done remarkably well or the mother has been a success in business, and so children have a lot of pressure on them to do well. We need to make sure that we love them, and not just love them but remind them how much we love them, remind them how much we care about them, how important they are, and how deserving they are of everything that's great.

That doesn't mean, though, that we can't "be the dad" or "be the mom" sometimes and maintain discipline. In other words, we also need to teach our kids to do chores at home. It's very important that they do that so they have a sense of self and a sense of responsibility. That unfortunately in my personal opinion is missing in our culture here in America. Unlike my own culture back in my native Ireland, where as kids we had chores, we had to work on the farm, we had to do things around the house. That doesn't seem to happen so much here in this country. That's something that I feel we're missing.

We also have to make sure that kids have great family values. That they're brought up with a degree of faith, whatever that is for your family, that they're taught respect and honor, and they're taught to live a life that's honest, that's full of integrity, that's joyous, that's healthy, that's happy. And unfortunately, we also need to help our children understand the dangers of drugs and alcohol and how devastating that can be not only for themselves but also for their families.

Children can develop a strong sense of self when they receive the support and encouragement that a stable, secure family can provide. "Family traditions are a sound way to foster a sense of stability and security and this contributes to the emotional health, self-esteem, and self-respect of family members. The family serves as the model for all interpersonal relationships," Dr. Brenner declares. "The way an individual is cared for, supported, encouraged, allowed to express and be themselves in the family, or not, enormously influences the choices and decisions an individual makes moving into the future."

It's important that we have discipline in the home as it relates to raising a family but over-disciplining is not good and under-disciplining is not good. It needs to be just a right balance. Kids need to be praised but they also need to have structure and they need to have a balance of discipline, honor, and respect, which seems to have gone out the window in some of the family values not only here in this country but around the world. I regularly witness kids talking back to their parents, talking back to their elders, talking back to people on the street, talking back to people at shopping centers, fighting and arguing amongst each other, "Oh, she got this" and "He didn't get that." There's a lack of control among children. One reason for that is that children who are well disciplined tend to come from good, stable families and we seem to be suffering from a shortage of those these days. As we saw in the first chapter, the numbers are staggering as it relates to separation or divorce here in this country—70 percent I believe of all marriages end in divorce and up to 50 percent of second marriages end in divorce so there are a lot of broken homes here in this country. As a result, the children are not disciplined properly. The nanny doesn't have the control or the authority or is never given the control by the parents consequently as a result, children are allowed to do whatever they want to do.

So it's very important that children are disciplined in the proper way. But at the same time they need to be praised and told that they are magnificent, that they are valued, that they are loved, and that they are good, worthwhile human beings who are going to go on to do marvelous things. It's very important that we praise our children. Children don't get enough praise. Quite the opposite, they are constantly criticized. Parents complain about their children all the time. Sometimes they are justified in doing so but when it's warranted they should be complimenting their children, telling them how good they are. Once a child is told they are great, they are worthwhile, they make a difference, "I'm proud of you," "I love you," "I think the world of you," it will really resonate with them and as a result, they will start to feel good. When their self esteem is raised they're able to perform better academically, mentally, emotionally, and physically.

Through it all, though, don't neglect your relationship with your partner. After all, it started with just the two of you, and from time to time you need to rekindle that intimate connection of just being a couple. Taking issue with some other relationship experts who suggest that it's not possible for couples to maintain a balance between their relationship and their parenthood, Dr. Gottman declares, "marriage and family are not so diametrically opposed. Rather, they are of one cloth." This is especially true for couples with infants. "Yes, the couple should spend time away from the baby occasionally," he writes. "But if they are making this transition well together, they will find that they can't stop talking about the baby, nor do they want to. They might not even get through that first meal without calling home—at least twice."

When that happens, couples can often be made to feel guilty by their perception of the expectations of others, he says, as if they're overly obsessed by their child at the expense of their relationship. "The result is that they feel all the more stressed and confused. But in fact, they have done something very right. The important thing here is that they are in it together. To the extent that both husband and wife make this philosophical shift, the parent-child relationship and their marriage thrive."

The needs of a vulnerable baby are necessarily paramount, but parents need to be sure that they "carve out time for the two of you," Dr. Gottman advises, advising couples to "use a baby-sitter, a relative, or friend to get some time alone with each other. But remember," he cautions, "you haven't failed if you end up spending a lot of your 'dates' discussing the baby—you've succeeded. As the baby grows into a toddler and then becomes school-aged, you'll find that your conversations when you're alone together won't always gravitate toward your child and your role as parents."

Before the child is born, a good way to prepare for this major change, he offers, is for the partners to concentrate on their relationship by making "sure that you really know each other and your respective worlds intimately. The more of a team you are now, the easier the transition will be. If a husband knows his wife, he will be in better tune with her as she begins her journey to motherhood."

Another good policy once the baby arrives is to make caring for it a true partnership, he suggests. "Sometimes in her exuberance, a new mother comes off as a know-it-all to her husband. While she pays lip service to the idea that they should share the baby's care, she casts herself into a supervisory role, constantly directing—if not ordering—the new father and even chastising him if he doesn't do things exactly her way. 'Don't hold her like that,' 'You didn't burp him enough,' 'The bath water's too cold.' In the face of this barrage, some husbands are more than happy to withdraw, to cede the role of expert to their wives (after all, their own fathers never knew anything about babies, either) and accept their own incompetence. The sad result is that they do less and less and therefore become less and less accomplished and confident in caring for their own child. Inevitably, they begin to feel more excluded."

That's a situation that's sure to drive a wedge between the partners, and thus, should be avoided. A good way to prevent that situation is for for the new mother "to back off," Dr. Gottman insists. "She needs to realize that there's more than one way to burp a baby. If she doesn't like her husband's way, she should remember that the baby is his child too and will benefit from experiencing more than one parenting style. A few baths in tepid water are a small price for an infant—and a marriage—to pay for the father's ongoing commitment to his family. If the mother feels her husband's approach is really unsafe, she should direct him to their pediatrician, Dr. Spock's tome, or some other edifying baby-care guide." Most of the time, however, the only thing wrong with the husband's approach is that it's not the same as the wife's. When that is the case, "some small, well-timed doses of gentle advice-giving are fine (don't forget to use a softened startup), but lectures and criticism will backfire."

He cautions that a particular challenge for new fathers is dealing with the complexities (not to mention mess!) of baby's mealtime. "Penis envy may well be a Freudian myth, but breast envy is alive and well in almost every home where the wife is nursing an infant. Fathers can't help but feel jealous when they see that a beautiful bond develops between their wife and baby. It's as if the two have formed a charmed circle that he just can't enter. In response to this need, some baby-care catalogs actually offer devices that allow men a close approximation of the nursing experience. There is, for example, an attachment that you can strap onto your chest that delivers warm milk to the baby through plastic breasts!"

Rather than take that extreme, and dubiously sensible, step, the majority of parents will seek other more natural methods of inclusion for the father, Dr. Gottman says. "Instead they can find a role for the husband in the ritual of breastfeeding. For example, it can be the husband's job to carry the baby to the mother at feeding time. He can also be the official 'burper.' He could also make it his custom to sit quietly with his wife and child during feeding times, gently stroking the baby's head, for example, or singing to his baby."

Generally it's not really possible, at least in the opinion of a lot of men, for the father to feel a connection with his child until after the youngster has become capable of physical interaction. "Unfortunately," Dr. Gottman comments, "by then their distance from family life has created fissures in their marriage. The reason men may take longer to 'bond' with their children is that, as countless studies have confirmed, women tend to be more nurturing toward children while men are more playful. And since most men assume you can't really play with a helpless baby, they don't feel engaged by their child for much of the crucial first year."

He declares that those fathers who make the effort to spend time with their babies may well be surprised by how responsive their baby can be after all and thus will reap the reward of an earlier, stronger, more meaningful bond with their child. These fathers will learn that their babies "are not 'blobs' who do nothing but cry, nurse, poop, and sleep. Even newborns can be great playmates. Babies begin to smile at a mere three weeks. Even earlier than that they can track movements with their eyes. Soon they are chortling, kicking their legs in delight. In short, the father who gets to know his babies by bathing, diapering, and feeding them will inevitably find that they love to play with him and that he has a special role in their lives."

The "new" husband that Dr. Gottman describes "is likely to make his career less of a priority than his family life because his definition of success has been revised." He thereby strengthens his relationship with his wife. "Unlike husbands before him . . . he makes a detailed map of his wife's world. He keeps in touch with his admiration and fondness for her, and he communicates it by turning toward her in his daily actions."

His wife benefits from this, of course, but so do the children. "Research shows that a husband who can accept influence from his wife also tends to be an outstanding father. He is familiar with his children's world and knows all about their friends and their fears. Because he is not afraid of emotions, he teaches his children to respect their own feelings—and themselves." As we saw earlier in this book, he is willing to switch off the TV—even if there's an important baseball or football game on—when his wife needs his attention. He will extend the same courtesy to his children too, he writes, "because he wants them to remember him as having had time for them."

A new baby will place what will seem to be limitless demands on the wife that could make even Dr. Gottman's "new" husband, with his "philosophical shift toward parenthood," feel a little deprived if not somewhat resentful. "Even if, intellectually, he understands that the baby's needs supplant his own in priority, he's going to miss his wife," he points out. "The more the wife acknowledges what he has given up and lets him know how central he still is to her life, the more understanding and supportive he will be able to be. If she never has any time for just the marriage, he will have a tendency to withdraw from the relationship."

The flip side to that issue of course, he adds, is that mom is "likely to be exhausted" by those apparently limitless demands, and could use—and would really appreciate—any assistance her husband can provide. Therefore, their relationship will greatly benefit "if her husband will modify his work hours so he can come home earlier and on the weekends take over for her now and then so that she can get a needed break to sleep, see a friend or a movie, or do whatever else she needs to feel part of the world again."

By working together in this manner, couples can experience a newfound intimacy and appreciation of each other and may discover to their amazement that "parenthood doesn't drag down their relationship" after all, Dr. Gottman suggests, but will in fact build it up.

So we've seen that the addition to children to a relationship, though a game changer, is certainly not game over. Indeed, working together in true partnership can deepen and enrich the relationship between two partners. In this chapter we've learned how to include the kids and plan family activities, but to never forget that you're still a couple. But what about when couples just can't resolve their differences and the family unit breaks up? It's an unfortunate situation for all concerned, but it can be survived, as we'll see in the next chapter.

CHAPTER 10

SINGLE PARENTING: SURVIVING THE STRUGGLE

Single moms and dads certainly have their work cut out for them as it relates to trying to parent on their own. Doing all the things one has to do to raise a family, including preparing meals and tending to your children's needs, can be a significant challenge for any parent, never mind a single parent, be it male or indeed, female. The key is can you find the time, particularly when being a single parent means that there is an exorbitant amount of pressure that one has to absorb as it relates to getting up in the morning, preparing meals, depending of course on the number of children the single parent has. This takes up a monumental amount of time and is a giant task not only for a single parent but also for a husband and wife. It all comes down to: "How can I cope with this situation to the best of my ability?" "How can I help raise a child or children that turn out to be happy and healthy human beings?"

One of the keys is to make sure that you have open dialog and close contact with your ex-spouse so that communication and connection, issues, challenges, hurdles, obstacles can all be overcome in a meaningful way in the best interest of the child or children. Unfortunately, many spouses argue over who should have custody over the child or children and this causes significant pain for everybody involved, especially for the child or children. Research indicates that children from dysfunctional or broken homes tend to have dysfunctional relationships themselves as it relates to not only dating but also marriage based on what they observed with his or her own parents.

So one of the keys is to communicate effectively. Let the children know that they are loved deeply by both parents in spite, on many occasions, of negative circumstances that are shown by either party to each other. In other words, what I'm trying to say is the parents can fall into this "he-said, she-said" kind of trap where many times one parent wants one thing, the other wants another and it winds up being a power struggle. Parental struggle seems to be a huge issue after a divorce. The most significant thing that both parents need to understand is that if there's a child or children involved, it is up to the adults to insure that emotional intensity, drama, conflict, and fights, are minimized for the benefit of the child or children.

Kids are masters at manipulation, they're either mommy's boy or daddy's boy, but they're not the only ones. Parents unfortunately pit themselves against each other and on many occasions they'll also pit the children against each other and engage in the blame game to seek advantage.

Child and family policy expert Edward Kruk wrote an insightful article on the subject titled, "The Impact of Parental Alienation on Children," which was posted on the website of *Psychology Today* magazine. "What children of divorce most want and need is to maintain healthy and strong relationships with both of their parents, and to be shielded from their parents' conflicts," declares Dr. Kruk, an associate professor of social work at the University British Columbia. He notes that sometimes parents, in an effort to compensate for their own personal insecurities, will make their children feel like they need to choose sides in their parents' dispute. "In more extreme cases, children are manipulated by one parent to hate the other, despite children's innate desire to love and be loved by both their parents."

These parents, Dr. Kruk states, are selfishly trying to instill their children with what has been termed "parental alienation" against the other parent in an attempt damage their relationship with them and trying to program them to view that parent in an undesirable light. This, he says, "is often a sign of a parent's inability to separate from the couple conflict and focus on the needs of the child. Such denigration results in the child's emotional rejection of the targeted parent, and the loss of a capable and loving parent from the life of the child."

A psychiatrist named Richard Gardner, Dr. Kruk relates, "developed the concept of 'parental alienation syndrome' twenty years ago, defining it as 'a disorder that arises primarily in the context of child custody disputes. Its primary manifestation is the child's campaign of denigration against a parent, a campaign that has no justification. It results from the combination of a programming (brainwashing) parent's indoctrinations and the child's own contributions to the vilification of the target parent.'" As a result, the children can develop such overwhelmingly adverse opinions about the targeted parent "that the parent is demonized and seen as evil."

Dr. Kruk also cites the work of Amy Baker, who wrote that "parental alienation involves a set of strategies, including bad-mouthing the other parent, limiting contact with that parent, erasing the other parent from the life and mind of the child (forbidding discussion and pictures of the other parent), forcing the child to reject the other parent, creating the impression that the other parent is dangerous, forcing the child to choose between the parents by means of threats of withdrawal of affection, and belittling and limiting contact with the extended family of the targeted parent."

In his own study of what happens when parents who lack custody become estranged from their children's lives, "I found that most lost contact involuntarily, many as a result of parental alienation," he writes. "Constructive alternatives to adversarial methods of reconnecting with their children were rarely available to these alienated parents," he adds.

The condition occurs more frequently than many would think, Dr. Kruk reports, commenting that a 2010 study revealed "both an increasing incidence and increased judicial findings of parental alienation." The condition may be present in as many as 15 percent of divorces in which children are involved, the study indicated. Other research indicates that parental alienation has been experienced by around 1 percent of North American adolescent children.

There is further research, he says, which supports the view that when taken to extremes, such treatment constitutes child abuse. It can frequently go unnoticed or unreported, though, "as child welfare and divorce practitioners are often unaware of or minimize its extent," he writes. "As reported by adult children of divorce, the tactics of alienating parents are tantamount to extreme psychological maltreatment of children, including spurning, terrorizing, isolating, corrupting or exploiting, and denying emotional responsiveness," he says, quoting Dr. Baker's research.

Indeed, instilling a child with "a false belief that the alienated parent is a dangerous and unworthy parent" can produce "a serious mental condition," he declares. "The severe effects of parental alienation on children are well documented; low self esteem and self hatred, lack of trust, depression, and substance abuse and other forms of addiction are widespread, as children lose the capacity to give and accept love from a parent. Self hatred is particularly disturbing among affected children, as children internalize the hatred targeted toward the alienated parent. Their depression is rooted in feelings of being unloved by one of their parents, and from separation from that parent, while being denied the opportunity to mourn the loss of the parent, or to even talk about the parent. Alienated children typically have conflicted or distant relationships with the alienating parent also, and are at high risk of becoming alienated from their own children. Baker reports that fully half of the respondents in her study of adult children who had experienced alienation as children were alienated from their own children."

Dr. Kruk continues, "Every child has a fundamental right and need for an unthreatened and loving relationship with both parents, and to be denied that right by one parent without sufficient justification such as abuse or neglect, is in itself a form of child abuse. Since it is the child who is being violated by a parent's alienating behaviors, it is the child who is being alienated from the other parent. Children who have undergone forced separation from one of their parents in the absence of abuse, including cases of parental alienation, are highly subject to post-traumatic stress, and reunification efforts in these cases should proceed carefully and with sensitivity (research has shown that many alienated children can transform quickly from refusing or staunchly resisting the rejected parent to being able to show and receive love from that parent, followed by an equally swift shift back to the alienated position when back in the orbit of the alienating parent; alienated children seem to have a secret wish for someone to call their bluff, compelling them to reconnect with the parent they claim to hate)," he points out. "While children's stated wishes regarding parental contact in contested custody should be considered, they should not by determinative, especially in suspected cases of alienation."

Children have to be shown how to hate as it is not an emotion that is normally part of their nature, he explains. Therefore, "a parent who would teach a child to hate or fear the other parent represents a grave and persistent danger to the mental and emotional health of that child. Alienated children are no less damaged than other child victims of extreme conflict, such as child soldiers and other abducted children, who identify with their tormentors to avoid pain and maintain a relationship with them, however abusive that relationship may be."

That's simply not the way to go, and will only hurt the children. It is highly important that both parents refrain from taking sides. It is better to remain neutral, to lay the ground rules, and establish the values that are important for proper upbringing. It is also very important that the parents, even though they may be separated 100 percent of the time, nevertheless continue to support each other as it relates to the children's wellbeing.

The key is to be mindful, to understand, to communicate, and to love effectively in order to raise a child who will grow up to be sound of mind, who will be happy and kind not only to others but also to his future spouse or her future spouse, and who will not repeat the same mistakes that they observed in their parents' relationship.

"What children really want and need is to stay out of their parents' conflicts and to maintain healthy and strong relationships with both parents," writes Dr. Baker in her *Psychology Today* website article, "Helping Children Resist the Pressure to Choose One Parent Over the Other." She notes that there are four "capacities" that parents can help their children develop which will not only enable the children to more easily negotiate the thorny experience of their parents' separation, especially avoiding the corrosive tendency of regarding one parent as being "better" than the other, but will also serve them well in dealing with other life challenges they may face as well.

The first is to help children work on their critical thinking skills. "When children think critically, they are aware of their thoughts, where they came from, and are able to examine the reality of them and change them accordingly," says the director of research at the Vincent J. Fontana Center for Child Protection at the New York Foundling who has a PhD in developmental psychology from Teachers College of Columbia University. "This skill will help the child question his or her ideas about each parent (i.e., one is all good, one is all bad; one is always right, one is always wrong). If a child is using critical thinking skills, it is not likely that he or she can be programmed or brainwashed into rejecting one parent to please the other."

The second capacity children need to be helped to acquire is the ability to utilize analytical tools that will enable them to carefully consider their options. "When placed in a pressurized situation in which a child feels compelled to do as one parent asks (i.e., not spend time with the other parent, spy on that parent, and so forth), it is important for the child to slow down, not act right away, and consider his or her options," Dr. Baker informs. "Doing so can prevent the child from automatically doing what the alienating parent is asking."

Number three involves tapping into their inner wisdom by learning to listen to their own heart. "When children learn how to be true to themselves and their values," she declares, "it is not likely that they can be manipulated or convinced to do something that goes against their best interest (i.e., cut off one parent to please the other) or something that betrays the other parent. Children need to be encouraged to identify their core values and to be attuned to when they are going against them."

Finally, parents can help their children deal with difficult situations by instilling in them effective coping skills and by letting them know how to seek out support. "Children sometimes feel that they are the only ones who are dealing with a problem and that no one can understand what they are going through," explains Dr. Baker. "Encouraging children to talk to other people such as friends, teachers, and other caring adults can help them feel less alone and can help them benefit from the wisdom and kindness of others. Children also have more internal resources (self talk, relaxation strategies) that they can develop and rely on in times of need."

One innovative strategy for helping children cope with the reality of their parents' separation is "bird's nest co-parenting." Though not practical for everyone, bird's nest co-parenting can be an effective solution in some cases, writes Dr. Kruk in another article, "Bird's Next Co-parenting Arrangements." This "uniquely child-centered" strategy involves having the kids remain in the family home and the divorced parents alternate between living with them "like birds alighting and departing the 'nest.'" It is an approach in which the parents selflessly put the needs and interests of the children first.

Calling it "a novel yet sensible arrangement," he says the parents can either live in separate housing when they are not in the family home, or can switch off living in an alternate accommodation as well. This way, "children experience much less disruption in their lives and routines than having to shuttle and adapt to completely new living arrangements. It can be either a semi-permanent or temporary arrangement, to allow children a smoother transition to life as a divorced family." And it makes sense because after all, the children are the innocent parties in this situation, it's the adults who decided they could no longer live together.

This approach is most effective when the parents are sharing the parenting duties equally, he notes, rather than just one devoting full time to caregiving. "The expense is another factor, depending on whether parents arrange for one or two residences away from the family home. If the former, bird-nesting need not be any more expensive than parents living in two separate households. It may even be less expensive than maintaining two homes for the children, as the external residence may be much more modest if the children are not residing there; a one-bedroom apartment or studio is likely to provide more than enough space. In addition, parents do not have to purchase two sets of toys and clothing for the children as they would if children were rotating between two households."

Another complication would be if one or both parent begins having other relationships. "In particular, privacy may become a serious issue of concern for one or both parents since the other parent's ongoing presence is obvious and unavoidable."

For bird nesting to function effectively, both partners will need to set aside their differences, at least when they're around the family house with the kids, but then, they should do that anyway. "Both need to maintain a certain level of consistency of purpose, discipline, and child-raising techniques to make it work well; this means being able to communicate clearly and peacefully rather than taking each discussion as an opportunity to argue," Dr. Kruk recommends. "Household and house maintenance arrangements, and ground rules, must be absolutely clear, and each parent must closely stick to the agreed-upon arrangements; over time, as they settle into the new lifestyle, more flexible arrangements are possible."

A mutually agreed-upon written plan for managing the arrangement is crucial to its success, at least early on, and working together to draw one up would be good activity for parents. "Ongoing mutual respect is vital; and although it is reasonable to assume that there will be arguments or disagreements about various aspects of the arrangement, it is critical that children are shielded from ongoing conflict."

Families aren't going to want to maintain the bird's nest model indefinitely, and a good time to end it, he suggests, would be when the oldest child turns eighteen "at which time one parent may either buy the other out of their interest in the family home, or it is sold and the proceeds divided pursuant to the matrimonial property regime or separation agreement." It would be nice to think— and it's at least possible—that the cooperation that has taken place during that time will lead the parents to settle all their differences and reunite.

Even if the differences are too great to resolve, at least during the time that the family continues the arrangement the kids will have a relatively stable environment. "They remain in the family home, their school and neighborhood friendships can continue uninterrupted, and of course they are able to maintain meaningful relationships with both parents, which is crucial to their ongoing well-being," Dr. Kruk writes.

Choosing to pursue this difficult approach is a highly praiseworthy thing for parents to do, he declares, "as they are clearly placing their children's needs and their responsibilities to those needs above their own interests. And the level of discomfort they are likely to experience may be significant, especially in light of their desire to have complete independence from their former spouse. Yet as more parents recognize that bird nesting is clearly the best arrangement for their children, the number of bird nesters is steadily rising."

One of the biggest challenges that divorced men and women are faced with is making the decision whether to enter into another relationship, one that might not work, based on how it went last time. It can be daunting to re-enter the dating game and see what's out there, all in the hope that this time they will meet the right person of his or her dreams. There's obviously going to be fear, trepidation, rejection, failure, low self esteem, uncertainty over self worth, worry about not looking good enough, doubts about how one competes in the dating game and where to go. There's a huge issue, particularly for women, as it relates to dating after a failed marriage or indeed, a long-term relationship that did not work out. It can be a challenge, but it's not impossible. In fact, it's exciting.

One way for a woman to alleviate some of the sensitivity or eliminate some of the apprehension surrounding dating is to ask a couple of girlfriends to join you on a night out. Go out and socialize with a group of friends. Maybe one of the friends has someone that they can ask, "How would you like to go out and date one of my friends?" And that's probably a safer bet—dating someone that you know or that a good friend knows rather than dating someone totally unknown to you. And many times great friendships can lead to unbelievable relationships just by a simple introduction through a friend. Your friend may have no interest in a particular guy or girl, but they may think that person would make a good match for you. It's probably best to date that way.

Many people go to dating sites and though some of them have been successful, it's not personally what I recommend. I've always felt that a good way to meet people is to simply bump into someone at the grocery store or at the gas pump, someone you either know or have a connection with or take an instant liking to. That can be a source, a spark, if you will, of connecting with someone, perhaps a person who lives in your neighborhood or, as we say in dating, who is convenient and geographically desirable.

People meet in the strangest places and we never know where Mr. Right might be. He might be someone you meet in a parking lot, he might be a person you happen to connect with in a grocery store or he might be in an electronics store. He could be your real estate person or perhaps your insurance man, you never know. You can't predict who is going to be Mr. Right for you, whether it's someone you meet through your church, your friends—it's always a safe bet to go that route. And take it easy and tread softly and wait and see what happens, but nevertheless, get out, socialize, and network, because we have social needs. We all need meaning and purpose in life, we all have the innate intelligence and capability of connecting with others, and the key is once you go out several times, you'll get in the swing of it and you'll eventually start to meet people. You'll start to enjoy yourself, you'll start to have fun. That's how life was meant to be in the first place—joyous and fun.

You need to bring back more joy in your life if your relationship has gone south. You deserve it. You deserve joy, you deserve beauty, you deserve to get dressed up, you deserve to go out, you deserve to have fun. You're a mother, you're a father, you're a single mom, you're a single dad, you deserve to get out and bring joy back into your life again. Everybody deserves happiness. The key is to make the decision and start over. No one's ever sure of what the outcome might be, but at least give it a try.

As we've seen, divorce and separation rates in this country are exceedingly high, and in second marriages divorce is also exceptionally high. We need to find common ground. We need to honor each other. We need to respect each other. We need to communicate and reduce conflict dramatically if we are to start a new relationship and make it stick this time. There are many driving forces that make relationships work and then there are many driving forces that, unfortunately, allow relationships to fall apart. One of the keys is to find someone that you love to spend time with, someone that doesn't find fault with everything you do, who is not bossy, who is not controlling, who doesn't like conflict—though conflict sometimes can be effective in some relationships because you don't want someone who is a yes person all the time. But you want to be able to find someone that respects you, that loves you for who you are, that doesn't want to change you, and who you don't want to change either.

I have found in my research as a clinical psychologist that the relationships which seem to work the best, the ones that are very effective, and joyous, and healthy and happy, are ones where there's utmost respect for each other, where there's a sparkle in the eye towards the other person. These are the relationships where the couple tend to do things together. They go shopping, go to the movies together, play sports together, are very active together. They also take breaks from each other to allow each other to rekindle the love and joy they first experienced when they first met.

Men don't like controlling women and women don't like controlling men. So we need to see if we can find a way to not control each other, and to allow each person to simply be, without being bossy, without being badgered, without being told what to do, without nagging. Men just need to understand that women are very, very sensitive. They need help, they need support, they need guidance, and all you have to do, ladies, is to ask a man for help. Ask a man to help you around the house and he'll gladly do it. Don't ask him in the middle of his favorite baseball game or football game or basketball game, ask him when it is appropriate. But do ask, and he will gladly do so.

Many women tend to try to do it all on their own. They take on the manly role, where they're wearing both the pants and the skirt at the same time. That's not conducive to a good relationship. We have to find a way to achieve balance in our relationships and one way to do so is to allow the man to be the man. And gentlemen, you need to allow the woman to be the woman of the house. Let her do what she needs to do, what she needs to do best, and let the man do what he needs to do best which technically is to be a provider, a security net, a gladiator, if you will, that's there to provide the family with security, to protect the family, to provide for the family, and to be there in a loving, kind, supportive way.

Women sometimes need to take a deep breath and not be so controlling and not be so badgering and combative on a continuous basis. If you fail to rein this in, you'll find that yours will be a very conflictual relationship with your new partner and you will likely, as they say, come apart at the seams, which usually means that a divorce is imminent. In relationships where there is constant badgering, there can be continual fighting and arguments, not only between parents and couples, but also with the children. Women need to know that they must be loyal and they must align themselves with their partners if they are to secure a very strong relationship. By not doing so, most relationships will end up in separation. It's very important that women understand this.

Once you have found that balance and successfully established a new relationship, if there are children from your previous relationship you'll need to decide when to introduce them to your new partner. I believe that men are less conservative than women in introducing their kids to a new girlfriend. Women are extremely cautious about introducing a new partner to their kids. They tend to wait much, much longer. They need to feel secure and the children need to feel secure.

A lot of the time children are angry at their mom and dad. In fact most of the time many of the kids are exceptionally angry that the relationship that their parents had did not work out. There is a tremendous amount of anger expressed by many of the kids, or maybe one more than the other. The blame may be apportioned to the father or indeed to the mother. They may have the attitude of "How dare you bring someone else into this relationship." It's a very sensitive issue.

It's a very compelling matter for many couples when they separate: when should they bring in the children or introduce the children to another partner. It's a profoundly sensitive move and there's no established timeframe on when it should take place. Generally if it happens, it can be in six months or it can be ten months. I've known many, many females who have still not introduced their partners at all due to the fact that they didn't want a backlash and don't want to end up losing the love and respect of their kids through the fact of introducing a new partner.

So there's no time period on it, it's strictly an individual choice how soon you introduce the kids. The problem is, if the relationship doesn't work out when the children are introduced to a new partner, there can be more anger, there can be more guilt, there can be more dissent. It can be a difficult situation for bringing new partners in and out of a child's life because it tends to show a lack of stability. The fact is, sometimes relationships just simply don't work out because the new partner may not want children and so then the children feel rejected. It's a very sensitive issue, so we have to be very cautious and very careful of that.

I would say that in general, a good waiting period would be six months to a year. Then you could broach the subject and tell your children that you've found someone that you really like. I would encourage children and single parents, separated parents, to go out with their new partner and with the kids after about five or six months just to see how they all get along, see how they connect. After all it's your relationship with them too. It certainly takes time—so that six-month to one-year period would definitely be good. You have to be very, very sure and secure about your relationship before, of course, you introduce the kids to your new partner.

It's absolutely a later rather than sooner proposition. Many spouses, unfortunately, jump in with a new partner very, very quickly, only to find that it's not working out and then they feel guilty and the kids feel guilty. Maybe the kids really, really liked the new person that you started to date and you have to come to them and say, "Well, it hasn't worked out." And of course, it hadn't worked out with mom either and so then all of a sudden they'll actually start pointing the finger at you. So it's a very delicate topic, a very delicate subject, a very delicate, sensitive issue.

In this chapter we've discussed the repercussions of divorce or the dissolution of a longstanding relationship and strategies for getting through it and getting on with your life. These are important skills, no doubt. But while it's true that some relationships simply can't be salvaged (or maybe just shouldn't have happened in the first place), your ultimate goal should be to keep things together and make it work if at all possible—that's certainly the primary focus of this book. So in the next and final chapter, we will look at ways to recover from what you may have thought would be an insurmountable impasse, make up, and maintain an enduring, rich, rewarding, fulfilling relationship.

CHAPTER 11

RECONCILING
CAN BE BEAUTIFUL

Reconciling can be beautiful and very therapeutic for both parties. We need to seek forgiveness and we need to be forgiven if things don't go the way we anticipated. You know, relationships can fall apart when one party becomes dissatisfied with something the other person has done. And it may not be pleasing to the other party so consequently as a result, many relationships go south.

We have, unfortunately, all-or-nothing-type thinking in many relationships which means that either party can cut each other off at any one particular time just because they didn't get their way. We have egocentric minds and we are very stubborn. We are set in our ways and bound by our perspectives and we can become exceptionally difficult sometimes. We may be going through emotional stress, financial stress, physical stress. We may have gone through a previous break-up and we don't want to go through another break-up.

There's a lot of instability when it comes to relationships but reconciling can be beautiful and exceptionally loving and kind, and it can be tremendously therapeutic to the body and the mind and the spirit of either party when we allow ourselves to surrender and come together. It takes a very strong person to do that. It takes a person who is willing to step up and let the other person know how much he or she loves them in order for them to come back together.

That can be vital to surviving a situation John Gottman calls "gridlock" in his *Seven Principles*. He comments, "If you are hopelessly gridlocked over a problem that just can't be solved, it can be cold comfort to know that other couples handle similar conflicts with aplomb, treating them the way they would a bad back or allergies. When you're stuck, trying to view your differences as a kind of psychological trick, knowing that you can learn to cope with this may at first seem impossible. But you can do it."

The first thing you need to do, he advises, is to change your expectations. For one thing, you can't "solve" the impasse, per se, but you can make it a subject of earnest negotiation. Whether it's something like a difference in religious belief or basic lifestyle habits, the disagreement over which you are gridlocked "will probably always be a perpetual issue in your marriage, but one day you will be able to talk about it without hurting each other. You will learn to live with the problem."

Dr. Gottman counsels that you both need to acknowledge the existence of the dispute and agree on what has brought it about. "Whether the issue is momentous, like which of your religions to pass on to your children, or ridiculous, like which way to fold dinner napkins, gridlock is a sign that you have dreams for your life that aren't being addressed or respected by each other. By dreams I mean hopes, aspirations, and wishes that are part of your identity and give purpose and meaning to your life."

Ranging from the practical, such as how much money to set aside for the future, to the philosophical, "dreams can operate at many different levels," he writes. "Often these deeper dreams remain hidden while the more mundane dreams piggyback on top of them and are easier to see. For example, underneath the dream to make a lot of money may be a deep need for security."

Given the fact that people can have separate dreams and that those dreams sometimes can be in conflict, the way to a successful relationship is through minimizing the differences and learning to live with them. "The happy couple understands that helping each other realize their dreams—to fully appreciate and respect their partner's life aspirations—is one of the goals of marriage," Dr. Gottman relates. "In happy marriages partners incorporate each other's goals into their concept of what their marriage is about. These goals can be as concrete as wanting to live in a certain kind of house or to get a certain academic degree. But they can also be intangible, such as wanting to feel safe or wanting to view life as a grand adventure."

The partners' goals may not only be different, they may be in direct opposition to each other. It could be a situation where a wife wants to attend college but her husband dislikes his high-paying job and wants to change careers which would affect their finances and make it difficult for them to be able to afford her tuition and expenses. "In a happy marriage, neither spouse insists or attempts to manipulate the other into giving up their dream. They work it out as a team. They fully take into account each other's wishes and desires."

So in the case of the college-bound wife, one solution may be for the husband to continue in his job for a few more years until she obtains her degree. In other words, "maybe practicality demands that one or both of their dreams be put on hold for a while. Whatever they decide to do isn't really the issue," according to Dr. Gottman. "The point is that their concept of their marriage incorporates supporting both of these dreams. The way they go about making such decisions—with mutual respect for and acknowledgment of each other's aspirations—is part of what makes their marriage meaningful to them. When either spouse doesn't fully appreciate the importance of supporting his or her partner's dreams, gridlock is almost inevitable."

If you have such a gridlock issue in your relationship, he suggests that you follow a procedure where you both sit down and write out as clear and concise a defense of your position as you can. "Don't criticize or blame your spouse," he instructs. "Don't bad-mouth each other. Instead . . . focus on what each partner needs, wants, and is feeling about the situation. Next, write the story of the hidden dreams that underlie your position. Explain where these dreams come from and why they are so meaningful to you."

An honest discussion of the issue can follow once the partners' positions have been written down. Dr. Gottman recommends that that process start with each person taking fifteen minutes to present their case while the other listens. Then switch places. "Do not try to solve this problem," he cautions. "Attempting to do that now is likely to backfire. Your goal is simply to understand why each of you feels so strongly about this issue."

Each speaker's presentation should consist of an earnest explanation of their dream, including a detailed description of it. "Explain where the dream comes from and what it symbolizes. Be clear and honest about what you want and why it is so important. Talk as if you were explaining your dream to a good friend or neutral third party. Don't try to censor or downplay your feelings about your dream in order to avoid hurting or arguing with your spouse. This is not the time to criticize or argue with your partner. How you feel about your spouse in relationship to this dream is a satellite issue that should not be addressed right now."

The listener must be attentive and non-judgmental. "Listen the way a friend would listen," Dr. Gottman says. "Don't take your spouse's dream personally even though it clashes with one of yours. Don't spend your time thinking up rebuttals or ways to solve the problem" and definitely don't be negative or state reasons why the dream can't be fulfilled. "Your role now is just to hear the dream and to encourage your spouse to explore it." When the speaker is done, say things like, "Tell me the story of that. I'd like to understand what it means to you."; "What do you believe about this issue?"; "What do you feel about it?"; "What do you want?"; "What do you need?"; "What do these things mean to you?"

Try to be as supportive as possible. "That doesn't necessarily mean that you believe the dream can or should be realized. There are three different levels of honoring your partner's dreams, all of which are beneficial to your marriage. The first is to express understanding of the dream and be interested in learning more about it even though you don't share it. The second level would be to offer financial support for the dream." The third level would be to participate in the dream with your spouse.

Clearly some of your spouse's dreams will be easier to go along with than others and there may be some you simply don't get. "That's O.K.," Dr. Gottman allows. "The bottom line in getting past gridlock is not necessarily to become a part of each other's dreams (although your marriage will be more enriched to the extent that you can) but to honor these dreams. After all, you don't want the kind of marriage in which you triumph at the expense of crushing your partner."

Once everything is out on the table, then you can begin the process of sorting it all out, recognizing where you differ, and coming to some sort of mutual starting agreement that can lead to an eventual resolution down the road. "Understand that your purpose is not to solve the conflict—it will probably never go away completely. Instead, the goal is to 'declaw' the issue, to try to remove the hurt so the problem stops being a source of great pain."

Now is the time to gently set limits of how far you are willing to compromise on the issue by defining "the minimal core areas that you cannot yield on," Dr. Gottman explains. "To do this you need to look deep into your heart and try to separate the issue into two categories. In one, put those aspects of the issue that you absolutely cannot give on without violating your basic needs or core values. In the second category put an aspect of the issue where you can be flexible because they are not so 'hot' for you. Try to make the second category as large as possible, and the first category as small as possible."

Go over your lists together and see where you may be able to make compromises, at least temporarily. Then write out a tentative plan that you both are willing to try on a limited basis. "It will be helpful if you also write a brief description of your ongoing conflict to confirm that you both understand it remains unresolved but can be lived with." Give that arrangement a two-month trial and "and then review where you stand. Don't expect this to solve the problem, only to help you both live with it more peacefully."

Don't expect this process to be a success on the first attempt. Indeed, "it may take more than one session to overcome gridlock on issues that have been deeply troubling to your marriage," Dr. Gottman says. "These sessions can be stressful, no matter how diligently you attempt to accept each other's viewpoint without judgment."

He suggests that couples finish the sessions "on a positive note" by selecting several of their partner's attributes that they find most appealing (their appearance, their kindness, their thoughtfulness, their generosity . . .) and thanking them. "The goal here is to try to re-create the spirit of thanksgiving, in which you count your blessings and look inward to express gratitude for all you have. This may be particularly difficult to do after talking about gridlocked marital conflict, but that's all the more reason to try."

As you gradually make progress, you'll appreciate each other's efforts more and more. "Be patient with the process," he counsels, "and each other. By their very nature, these problems are tenacious. To loosen their grip on your marriage will take commitment and faith on both your parts. You'll know you're making progress when the issue in question feels less loaded to you both—when you can discuss it with your sense of humor intact, and it no longer looms so large that it crowds out the love and joy in your relationship."

Many times it works when we try to get back together. Sometimes it does and sometimes it doesn't, but you know that there's an opportunity for you to reconcile and when both parties are open to that it can be a great thing. Even with marriages, I know many people who separated, reconciled, and got back together and re-married and have beautiful relationships now. They got it right the second or third time around. It takes practice, it takes time. And the same with just dating. We fight, we fall out, we have disagreements, and then we re-connect and that's a beautiful thing. We keep doing that and doing that and eventually it works or it doesn't work. So I think that couples need to plan more joy and more fun in their lives. Men need to be less controlling and women need to be less bossy. And if we can do that we'll have a better opportunity of finding someone we can have a joyous, loving relationship with.I have watched and observed so many relationships where the men tell the women that they can't go out with their friends or the girls are telling their young dates they can't do this, or they can't do that, or they can't hang around with certain people. They're setting the ground rules at such an early stage in their relationships that there's no opportunity for them to fall in love. There's no opportunity for them to have anything of decency or any form of connection in their relationships.

So sometimes we set the standards too high and we're too controlling. If we can be less controlling in our relationships we will have a better opportunity of finding someone that we can really, really have a joyous loving relationship with. We need to be more joyous, we need to be happier, we need to have less restrictions. We don't need to always have our seatbelt on so to speak, we need to break free and enjoy the moment, and that's what men and women look for.

You know, when you ask partners in relationships what it was that attracted them to each other, a lot of the time you'll see that their getting together was not even about each other's looks or the physicality or how sexy one or the other was, it was about how much fun that person had with the other person. If you ask a woman questions like, "Whatever attracted you to the person in the first place?" for instance, many will respond, "It was his personality, he was funny." I found this a lot based on my experience as a psychologist and author. Men and women are attracted to each other for different reasons. Sometimes it can be a physical attraction, but generally that doesn't last. Sometimes it does and again, sometimes it doesn't. But many of the times when you look at the big picture, you'll more often get answers like, "It's how much joy she brings me," or "It's about how much fun he is and how much joy I get when I spend time with this person because I can be myself." Men and women, we need to be ourselves and when we can be ourselves then we're free and when we're free, we can be happy. That's what we should be looking for in relationships: joy, fun, health, and happiness and fewer restrictions.

Men need to be strong. Women like that, they like men who are strong. Men like women who are strong as well, but also they like women who are very sexy and sensitive, which most women are. Ladies, we men need you to be sensitive, we need you to be sexy, but we don't want you to be controlling. If you're going to be controlling and your partner is controlling, then there is no opportunity at all for growth and there's no opportunity for moving forward because you want your way, he wants his way, and it becomes a wrestling match of who gets to win. That's just not how it should be. It should be a win-win situation for all parties concerned. So find a balance.

You know, you can still have your disagreements, but have them lovingly without being aggressive toward one another as I've shown you elsewhere in this book, and try to find a happy medium. I can tell you this: the better your self esteem is, the more you like yourself. The more you love yourself unconditionally in a very powerful, positive way for both parties, the better the opportunity will be for you to have a more powerful relationship. People who don't like themselves tend to think that their partner is stronger than they are. When they perceive their partner to be stronger than they are, they don't feel as comfortable in their own skin and they don't feel as powerful around them. As a result, that relationship can come apart and generally does.

That's when you need a solid strategy for getting things back together, writes Steven Stosny in his article, "Connection Repair: Strategy vs. Tactics and Maneuvers," posted on the *Psychology Today* website. Strategy is quite different from tactics and maneuvers, says Dr. Stosny, an expert on relationships who founded Compassion-Power outside of Washington, D.C., has conducted workshop all over the world, and who has written several books on relationships. "Strategy," he explains, "embodies what you want, tactics concern how to get what you want, and maneuvers are the actions you take to get what you want. Unless there is agreement on a strategy to repair the relationship, anything that either party does will seem like manipulation, no matter how benignly they might describe their efforts: e.g., trying to 'get my needs met' or 'communicate' or 'be fair' or 'hold you accountable.' This is not because either party is manipulative or controlling by nature; rather it's an unavoidable result when tactics and maneuvers supersede strategy."

When tactics and maneuvers endorsed by experts in the field don't work out, he says, they "are always blamed on the partner's 'insensitivity, selfishness, stubbornness, laziness, immorality, mental illness, or personality disorder,' thereby draining the life from any repair strategy, if not the relationship itself."

Probably the worst case of making strategy secondary to tactics and maneuvers, Dr. Stosny declares, "is the overemphasis on communication skills. Many therapists and self-help authors love these, because they are easy to describe, albeit almost impossible to enact effectively during heightened emotional arousal. But even when successful, they are likely to weaken a viable strategy of relationship repair. If you subscribe to communication skills as a cure for distressed relationships, ask yourself this: At those times when you felt heard in your relationship—when your communication skills worked— did you then feel closer, more connected, more valued? If not, your partner probably felt on some level that your 'communication' was an attempt to manipulate or control, when the real problem was tactics and maneuvers undermining the desire to repair."

But communication is important when the two of you discuss exactly what the nature of your relationship should be and your strategy for achieving it. This is a talk you need to have, he says. Once you've agreed on the definition and the strategy, then tactics and maneuvers can be applied "toward maximizing the agreed upon strategy and should never undermine or subvert it." And that's when good communication is crucial.

For some ten years, Dr. Stosny has been conducting what he calls "boot camps" at which couples in "highly stressed relationships" receive assistance in ways to develop individualized repair strategies. "Most of the 4,000-plus participants so far have chosen the first option, 13 percent go for the second, and 10 percent agree on the third."

The first strategy calls for couples to "build a connected, loving relationship, featuring teamwork, cooperation, equality, respect, compassion, kindness, affection, tolerance of differences, and mutual growth."

The second strategy suggests that the partners "build a companionate relationship of mutual respect and support."

The third strategy involves creating "compassionate co-parenting upon the dissolution of our relationship, which we have come to regard as too damaged."

Participants at the boot camps have come up with three main tactics for achieving any of the three strategies described above. The first involves "self-regulation skills," the second calls for the partners to "behave in accordance with your deeper values," and the third suggests the adoption of "binocular vision."

The "self-regulation skill," Dr. Stosny explains, "usually means the ability to regulate impulses and emotions sufficiently to act in your long-term interests (so you don't shoot yourself in the foot). I believe that self-regulation skills in love relationships must also include the ability to maintain self-value when we don't like our partners' behavior—so we do not feel devalued by it—and the ability to hold onto value for our partners, when we don't like their behavior or they don't like ours—so we don't devalue them. When tactics subvert strategy, both parties feel they can neither sustain self-value nor value for each other without getting their partner to do something. At best, this amplifies the emotional intensity that tends to lock couples in power struggles. At worst, one or both try to get compliance by making the other feel shame, fear, or anguish, which is a definition of emotional abuse."

One of the hardest times for us to rein ourselves in, he comments, is when we're upset with our partner for not doing what we want them to do and are trying to get them to change. In other words, when we're being too controlling. "It's wiser to focus on the emotional state we're in when we speak or act. Abundant evidence shows that people primarily react to the emotional tone of communication rather than the choice of words. These are non-verbal cues such as body language, tone of voice, facial expressions, tension, distractedness, hesitations, impatience, discomfort, eagerness, or enthusiasm, and behavioral impulses to approach, avoid, or attack. In fact, we most often react emotionally before the brain processes the meaning of the words. Thus good communication follows from self-regulation skills. But when couples try to put the cart before the horse, as many self-help authors imply they should ('You'll feel better when you express how you feel!'), attempts at communication undermine self-regulation: i.e.: both parties feel attacked (with their unregulated negative feelings as self-validating proof), while neither consciously intends to attack."

The benefits are significant and many when your actions remain in line with your personal convictions, Dr. Stosny feels, and include "authenticity, conviction," and "long-term wellbeing." On the other hand, "there are painful reminders for ignoring or violating our deepest values: guilt, shame, anxiety, regret, feeling inadequate, or unlovable—whenever we fail to be caring, compassionate, protective, or loyal to the people we love. Unfortunately, we tend to blame these reminders on our partners ('She's laying a guilt trip on me!'), instead of viewing them for what they are: motivations to remain true to our deeper values." This explains why it is that we can never expect to derive wellbeing from playing the blame game. In fact, taking that route, and acting at variance with our deeply held beliefs, will only increase our bad feelings.

Dr. Stosny defines the final tactic, binocular vision, as "the ability to hold our partner's perspectives alongside our own, see ourselves through our partner's eyes, and read our partner's reactions to understand and compensate for our blind spots, which are things we inadvertently do to undercut our interactions or harm our relationships. With binocular vision, the heart of communication is to understand the partner's perspective more fully, rather than control, manipulate, or negatively label it."

No matter how strong your opinion may be on an issue or how convinced you may be that you are right, if you can't at least put yourself in your partner's shoes and see why they feel the way they do—in other words, see things from their side—then you can never be sure that your position is the correct one. "Even if very accurate," he points out, "your perspective alone will provide an incomplete picture of your interactions. Worse, failure to see your partner's perspective will render yours far from correct, as the brain tends to fill in gaps in data with negative attributions. In other words, you will assume the worst about your partner. Negative attributions usually start out wrong but quickly become self-fulfilling, as they intensify emotional reactivity and make both partners behave at their worst."

Participants in his "boot camps," Dr. Stosny relates, are provided with training "in ways to develop new habits of self-regulation and interaction. Building new habits is crucial to repairing relationships, simply because well over 90 percent of emotional interactions between intimate partners, who live together for a significant period of time, run on autopilot, i.e., we tend to react the same way in the same contexts over and over. Under stress, habits dominate behavior. Due to state-dependent recall, when in aroused states, we're unlikely to remember what we learned in calm learning states. That's why Mr. Hyde can't recall what Dr. Jekyll learned in self-help books or communication therapy."

The wisdom of the ages is in the old saw, "You can't teach an old dog new tricks," for the most part, or at least it's a difficult and time-consuming endeavor, he declares. It requires "high motivation to practice new behaviors daily for a period of six weeks or so—the optimal time-frame for habituation." Therefore, the process of recovering from a strained or torn relationship cannot take place if you are not fully invested in the strategy to fix it.

"The best way to evaluate advice on relationship repair," Dr. Stosny concludes, "is to test whether the recommended tactics and maneuvers advance the strategy to which you and your partner have passionately committed. If not, they are likely to undermine and subvert it."

I feel that one of the key ways for us to keep our relationships together is for the partners to offer encouragement to each other. So the keys are to encourage each other, be loving to each other, be kind to one another, really listen to one another when the other person is talking—really pay attention. Most times, men either don't listen very well or women don't listen very well or don't hear what the other party is saying; it can work both ways. But if we can find a way to hear each other, understand each other, love each other, take off the seatbelts, and enjoy the journey, enjoy the moment, you will have created for yourself a great opportunity to love someone unconditionally. The greatest gift we can give each other is the gift of love and we should enjoy that.

Many of the factors that come out that cause relationships to break up are personal issues. Our difficulty in our relationship may really have nothing to do with the other person or any sort of clashes we're having with them, but may in fact involve just our own issues—with who we are as human beings. So a lot of the time in a relationship that's just not working out, it can be because one of the partners is dealing with unresolved personal issues. That's why I encourage people to go and seek therapy, to find a really good therapist who can help you understand why you're doing what you're doing, perhaps why you're causing the conflict in a relationship, and why the relationship is not working the way you would like it to work. And I encourage that for both men and for women, and also particularly for children as well if they have gone through a divorce.

I especially think everybody should go seek the advice of a therapist if they're contemplating walking away from a relationship. If things are stormy for you and your partner it may look good on the other side, but certainly from my experience it is not. If you look at the columns and columns of personal ads in most newspapers and magazines in this country you begin to get a picture of how many people are out of relationships. Likely many of them wish they had stuck it out in the one they were in.

It's pretty scary to have to go out and see if you can find someone either in a bar, restaurant, at the gym, dance hall, pub, or restaurant. It's particularly scary for women, maybe not so scary for men. A man can handle it a little more easily, but for a woman, it's a scary prospect. So divorce, separation, breakups, they can all be avoided if we literally just sit down and go see the therapist who can help you work out your differences. I think it's really important that people do that before they take the next step. Once you take that step, there's usually no turning back. That means trying to turn back from divorce and that's tough to do. And once you start down that road, it can happen two or three times because as we've seen, the likelihood of divorce increases with second and third marriages.

Like I've said, we all have personal issues, and we need to take a closer look at them. One of the things to look at is what the two partners in a relationship are bringing to the table—baggage if you will. What does he bring to the table? What does she bring to the table? Can we resolve our differences? Do we feel good about ourselves? Is our self esteem good? Do I feel adequate? Am I sensitive enough? Am I worthy? Are my children worthy? Am I worthy of him? Is she worthy of me? We have to look at the whole big picture.

There were good reasons you married in the first place; you have to look at all the reasons why you married this person. If you look at all the reasons and focus on the reasons why you married this person—because you liked them for whatever it was you liked them for: his looks, her build, his physicality, her eyes, the way he touched you, the way she kissed you—there's a good chance you'll be able to rekindle at least some of those feelings. In fact, I talked to a couple recently and I said, "What was it that attracted you to this man in the first place?" and she said, "It wasn't so much his good looks, but it was how he kissed me. That was the thing that made me feel so good about him, because he was so gentle with me."

All of these things are so important to a woman. Not so much so for a man, maybe, but women need sensitivity, they need to be heard, they need to be understood. Men also need to be heard and understood but not so much as women. So if we—meaning men— can find a way to be still and we can really relax, and be present, and be more mindful, and be more caring, and more sensitive, we'll have less friction and less conflict and a better quality of life. Men, we don't want you to be like women, we just want you to listen and be aware.

I've counseled tons and tons of people over the years and I've found, again, many of the issues that happen in relationships happen because of one's personal issues that spill over to the other person. This can happen, for example, when he or she is not really ready for a relationship though they really care about the other person. So I've found that people who have grown apart, who have separated for a couple of months, believe that they would love the other person unconditionally if only he would change or if only she would change. I have spent time with these people individually, getting their perspectives on things and their perceptions of how their relationships are going, and then allowed them to come together as couples to talk things out. I have them discuss how they really feel about each other and get them to reflect on some of the things they've said or done in the heat of the moment which perhaps didn't really reflect their true feelings. Often they are not even aware that these things were driving a wedge between them and their partner.

Many times we're just blinded. We are just not mindful, we're just not aware. Often the kinds of relationship problems we're talking about start to escalate from normal disagreements to outright conflict simply because we don't have the tools to deal with them. And this is why it's so important to equip ourselves with the kinds of skills that will help us relate to our partners. You know, a farmer needs his tools, a builder needs his tools, an electrician needs his tools for him to do the job properly. We as human beings, couples in relationships and marriages, particularly with children, need tools in order for us to be effective communicators.

I think a breakdown in communication is perhaps one of the biggest roadblocks to having purposeful, meaningful, joyous, happy, healthy, beautiful relationships. If you don't have the tools, you can certainly go get them and you should. Go to the therapist, go to the psychologist, go seek out someone—a marriage and child therapist—who has the tools and who can help you not only have a better relationship but also a better quality of life. I highly encourage that in all relationships.

Conflict is a huge issue. We see conflict with different religions, cultures, and ethnicities throughout the world, including warring between different countries, all because each country has a different point of view than the other country. We also see this on the individual level. In order for us to have a meaningful, joyous, purpose-driven life, we must find a way to communicate much more effectively—heart-to-heart, soul-to-soul, spirit-to-spirit. We must find a way to increase communication in order for us to reduce the conflict and misunderstanding, and we must find a way to lessen the hurt and love each other unconditionally, the way scripture intended.

Unfortunately, that is often not the case. Here in Los Angeles we have millions of cars on the freeway, just like every major city. This can be highly stressful if you are one of those cars stuck on your way home from work. I watch and observe conflict every single day: people driving their cars, people shouting, yelling, screaming obscenities at each other. Why do we do these things? We do these things because we have too much stress in our lives: We're not eating the right foods, our adrenals are completely shot, we don't take time to meditate or pray or give thanks for the gifts that we have at this very present moment in our lives. We're not thankful—we are out of control with our emotions; our hormones may be completely off; we certainly are not consuming the right types of food; and we're consuming lots of caffeine-laden drinks which also cause us to have emotional outbursts.

Reducing conflict, increasing communication, loving more, understanding our partners, and really, really listening—those are the keys, the tools, if you will. We are terrible listeners, both men as well as women, so when another party is not being heard, they tend to react. In my own personal life I know that when I'm not being heard, I tend to get very upset. And so I have to learn to breathe and just understand that perhaps the other person does not have the tools just yet. My job at that point is to share my feelings with them and give them an opportunity to hear my side too. By doing so, I am letting them know that if you really, really listened you would be able to hear exactly what I'm saying, so there would be less conflict, there would be more opportunity to connect, and more opportunity to have as loving and powerful a relationship as possible. That doesn't always happen, but when it does, it's wonderful.

And while reconciling should be your ultimate goal if you are having difficulties in your relationship, it's not something that can be bought at any price. You need to be flexible, you need to give, but you can't just simply yield to all your partner's whims. That's a solution that's bound to end in resentment and can't last. John Gray addresses that issue in *What You Can Feel, You Can Heal* when he writes, "To love a person doesn't mean you will always agree with them or even feel good about them. It doesn't mean you will like all of the things they do or don't do. Nobody is perfect. Whenever you like a person, there will always be some things you dislike too. And if you really love someone, it inevitably happens that sometimes you not only dislike what they do, but that you hate it. For most people, 'hate' is a dirty word. It's thought to be taboo to feel hate towards your partner. That's only allowed during the divorce proceedings."

But if you're indifferent towards a person, you're not going to have enough passion to hate it when they let you down. "Hate is really just a symptom of obstructed love," Dr. Gray declares. "When you love someone and they do something that is hard for you to love and accept, the natural reaction is to hate that behavior. You want to change that person so you can love them again."

If you try to suppress the resentment you're feeling towards a person, you'll wind up feeling hatred, he asserts. It's inevitable. "If you don't give yourself permission to express your hate in appropriate ways, it gets repressed, and along with it, you repress your ability to love fully."

Pent up feelings of anger or disappointment, left unexpressed, will come out eventually, likely in an outburst of alarming and unintended intensity. What can happen is that there will be a blow-up "or you may work very hard at repressing (your feelings) and think they are forgotten. They may be forgotten but they still have an effect—you are cursed to emotionally overreact in your relationships."

And that's too bad because really, it's not that hard to get those feelings of anger or disappointment out into the open and talk them over with your partner. "The only thing you need to do," Dr. Gray explains, "is tell the complete truth about them. Many people attempt to do this and find it doesn't work, because when they become angry their partner just becomes angry back. Getting angry back and forth makes it even more difficult for you to let go of the negative feelings and find the love and forgiveness."

One of Dr. Gray's favorite methods for getting those feelings out in a non-confrontational way is to state your position in what he calls a "love letter." For such a simple solution, it's amazingly potent. "Whenever you begin to notice your resentment, sit down and write a "Love Letter" to your partner," he advises. "Express all your anger and resentment, moving down through your hurt, fear, and guilt, and miraculously, a new rush of love will bubble up and you will be able to genuinely forgive your partner and be in love again."

You don't have to approve of what that person has done in order to forgive them, he says. "To forgive is to resolve your emotional resistance so that your love can flow as freely as it did before. To forgive is to give your love as before (for-give)."

Dr. Gray asserts that feelings of suppressed anger are so easily passed from person to person and so common among families that they practically qualify as an epidemic. "Unexpressed anger usually gets acted out through our behavior. You may end up taking out your frustration on some innocent bystander, or your wife and children, and they pass it along. Trying to be nice and kind by suppressing your negative feelings only allows them to build up until you either explode irrationally or you become so repressed that you have numbed your ability to feel positive emotions."

Once you have given expression to your feelings of frustration, rather than let them get bottled up, "you will naturally arrive at a feeling of forgiveness," he writes. "Forgiveness means an emotional acceptance of what happened. Now you can work towards preventing its repetition. It is a willingness to let go of what happened and find the love again—not forgetting about it, but expressing the resentment so that the emotional tension is dissolved, and then expressing your willingness to for-give."

In order for you to grow as a person, it is vital that you go through what Dr. Gray calls "the process of releasing your negative feelings and coming to a genuine state of love and forgiveness." He continues, "When you stop loving, it is you who suffers the most. When you hold on to anger and resentment, it is you who misses out on the love." You will experience a triumphant sensation of success when you are able to process and ultimately set aside your feelings of anger and resentment and give yourself over to feelings of love.

"By giving yourself permission to feel and heal your hate and negative emotions," he says, "the obstructed love inside can flow again. Expressing the negative feelings that come up in a relationship is not a sign of weakness or failure—on the contrary, it is a sign of strength that you are committed to resolving whatever negative emotions get in the way of your feeling in love all the time."

But there will be times when you are in the wrong—when you come to regret your "heat-of-the-moment" actions or words or when you've simply made a mistake. Then it's very important that we find an opportunity to apologize. I believe—this is my personal opinion—that it's vital to apologize as quickly as possible. For a man, his ego tends to get in the way and he generally takes longer to apologize than a woman. But for both men and women, the quicker we can apologize, the better, and the timing of when to apologize is very important. Doing it as quickly as possible gives us a better opportunity for reconnection, for restoring the verbal damage or the hurt and pain that happened due to being misunderstood or saying something that caused the other person pain.

John Gray comments, "Whenever there is an upset in your relationship, only one of you needs to apologize to make up. There is always something you can apologize for, even if you feel that your partner is more in the wrong. Simply saying you are sorry and that you want to make up is one of the most powerful statements to make." If you are able to develop the ability to swallow your pride just a bit and apologize from time to time, your relationship will benefit tremendously.

"If your partner apologizes to you and you are not ready to make up," he continues, "at least let him know you appreciate the apology. At this point the ball is in your court. It is up to you to process your issues so that you can finally let go and make up with your partner. It only slows down the healing process to justify staying hurt because our partner has not apologized or because he doesn't feel bad enough."

It is useful to again employ the letter-writing strategy here, Dr. Gray believes. "During a time-out, it may help you to let go of wounded feelings by writing a letter to yourself, saying the words you need to hear. Write out what you would want to hear to make you feel better. In this way, you are taking a step toward being responsible for feeling better. Read the letter and imagine how you would feel if your partner said or felt these things. Then write out what you would want to say in response By doing this, you are then free to feel your heart open once again."

Another thing you could do with the letter, he suggests, would be to present it to your partner and have him read it. If you think he'd be comfortable with it, you could even do a little role playing by having him read your letter out loud to you. Make your letter explicit and specific and don't be afraid to include words of praise for yourself if you honestly feel they are warranted, after all, this is your vision of what you would like him to say and be feeling towards you.

"Let him know these words would feel really good to you if he used them in his apology. If he can't say the exact words, try to appreciate what he can say. If you can't agree on what went wrong or who is wrong, agree that what happened is not what you wanted to happen, and that you want to make up and feel connected again."

Just like in a physical confrontation, emotional battles can have lasting effects. But just as bruises heal, so do emotional scars. "If we are waiting for our partners to provide us with a specific apology to help us heal, we are postponing our healing," Dr. Gray declares. "A child needs to hear an apology, but an adult can gradually learn to let go on his own. As adults, it is important to learn how to open our hearts again without waiting for our partners to take that step."

So the quicker the apology can happen, the better it is for both parties. For a man it can be done by giving a woman a flower and letting her know that you apologize, that you're sorry for what happened, that you'll work hard to make it right and not do the same thing again. It's important that one person in the party initiate an apology as quickly as possible. Many people, including many researchers and other experts in relationships, feel it's not necessary to do so, but I wholeheartedly believe that it's important that one party or the other take assertive action as quickly as possible. By doing so, then less time goes by and more joy can be created, more connections can be created rapidly. It's much better than waiting for a day or two days or a week during which you're running around with animosity towards your partner, because then if you haven't apologized, more conflict can ensue due to other issues that may come up during the week. So the quicker one apologizes the better it is and the faster one can develop more love and happiness. That's what the whole goal of the relationship and connections are all about—developing more love and joy and reducing conflict and reducing stress so that you have a better quality of life.

And even as we're having difficulties, we should take a measure of comfort in realizing that not only is conflict inevitable, it's actually healthy, provided we can work it out amicably. In *Love and Respect*, Emerson Eggerichs observes, "Along with research done by academics on connectivity, I also studied the scriptures and came upon a paradox: I learned that God intended for some conflict to exist in a marriage (I Corinthians, 7:3 & 4). Even secular research showed that the best marriage relationships had some conflict. It's almost as if you need a degree of conflict to keep the passion there. The sequence seems to have the couple experience a misunderstanding, they have a minor argument, a bump of some kind. But as they work through this conflict, they deepen their understanding of each other and value and appreciate one another all the more as they reconcile the conflict."

That doesn't mean there isn't some danger involved when problems do arise. "Obviously, when the sparks fly and a couple has a conflict, serious or minor, there is a risk. It can go one of two ways: sparks can cause a controllable fire that heats the house and makes things warm and comfortable, or sparks can set a wildfire that burns the house down. All married couples must realize that the sparks are going to be there. The question is, how will you control them? I talked with one husband who confessed that he tried to motivate his wife to show him some respect by acting very unlovingly. He distanced himself from her. He closed off his spirit in anger. He disregarded her feelings. He argued his points to win and never reconciled. In short, he never made peace with her. He admitted to me, 'I thought if I did all that, she'd start showing me a little more respect.' Then he put his head down on the table in despair and said, 'But she divorced me, and until now, I didn't know why.'"

Clearly that man lacked the communication skills necessary to keep the dialog going and sustain a healthy relationship. He didn't think that he and his wife could simply talk things over and come to some mutual agreement. But they can! "Husband and wife can work it out," Dr. Eggerichs insists. "As you have conflict, your wife will probably recognize it much sooner than you do. She can feel rejected by you in a way that you do not feel rejected by her (see Isiah 54:6). Consequently, she wants to have things resolved between the two of you, and she'll move toward you to get this done. As you go head-to-head and solve the problem, you become heart-to-heart. This is very precious to her. It's a very powerful thing for your wife when she knows that the two of you are at peace."

Trying to avoid all confrontation is clearly not the way to go, he cautions. "Don't refuse to make peace by running from conflict with your spouse. Conflict is not a sign you have a bad marriage. In fact the Bible says that those who marry "will have trouble" (Corinthians 7:28). What kind of trouble did Paul have in mind? Earlier in the section he lays down an excellent principle for dealing with conflict in marriage: the husband must fulfill his duty to his wife, and likewise also the wife to her husband. The wife does not have authority over her own body, but the husband does, and likewise also the husband does not have authority over his own body, but the wife does (I Corinthians 7:3 & 4)."

Paul's audience in this particular section, Dr. Eggerichs explains, was "couples in the church at Corinth. It was not uncommon in the first century for some believers to get the idea that a Christian would abstain from sex completely, and apparently that was what was going on at Corinth. To correct this error, Paul encourages sexual relations between husband and wife because this is the way not to fall into temptation and immorality outside of marriage. It seems a little odd, however, when Paul says that the wife doesn't have authority over her own body and the husband does and the husband doesn't have authority over his own body, the wife does. What does Paul mean? I believe he's laying out one of the great principles of the New Testament: because you have equal but differing needs, you will experience conflict." Nevertheless, these differences are manageable, he maintains, and can be resolved together.

"The husband should not act independently from his wife, and the wife should not act independently from her husband," Dr. Eggerichs writes. "A husband and wife should and can act together. It is as if God said, 'I'm going to allow for tension to exist in your marriage. I intend for you to work this out because as you work out your tensions, your relationship is going to deepen, and then deepen some more. And you're going to continue to go through life working it out, back and forth, back and forth.' "

So what we can do for ourselves and our relationships is listen more, love more, communicate better, reduce the conflict, exert less control, and release the brakes. You're not driving with your brakes on in this relationship, but many of us unfortunately feel like we are, as I've been told thousands and thousands of times. I work with couples to help them have a better quality of life, and when I listen to what they're saying and give them thoughtful responses, they know they're really being heard. They're not getting that from their relationship simply because one of the partners (or, indeed, both) doesn't have the tools.

It's just so important that you fine tune. Get your toolbox out, go to the seminars, go to the courses, attend family seminars on relationships which allow you to communicate better and have a more effective life and more love with your partner. This will bring more joy, health, and happiness into your life not only for you personally but also for your children if indeed children are involved.

Avoid negative expectations in your relationship. It is crucial that we develop a fresh vision for our lives together. Expect to live a victory. Have a can-do attitude. Your life follows the direction of your dominant thoughts. You can win with your thoughts.

So this is why abundance is important. You create abundance by the joy and the love and the compassion that you share with others. "Ask and you shall receive. Seek and you will find. Knock and it shall be opened for you." This is why it's important that you're aware. This is why it's important that you connect and communicate and that you integrate and you get along with not just your partner, but people in general. Have inner peace, be present. Be in the moment, your moment. Be thankful. Be joyous. Fill your mind and your body and your spirit full of love.

Bitterness will poison your heart and wreak havoc on your health. Make sure that, as Scripture says, no "root of bitterness shoots forth and causes trouble as many become contaminated by it." If you want to live in victory, you must harbor no ill against anyone. Out of the heart flows the issues of love. And remember, a bitter root will produce bitter fruit. Reach down and tear out those problematic roots and throw them away. They don't belong here. All they do is poison and pollute your life.

BIBLIOGRAPHY

GRAY, John
Men Are From Mars, Women Are From Venus
The Classic Guide To Understanding The Opposite Sex
HarperCollins (1992)

GRAY, John
Why Mars and Venus Collide
*Improving Relationships by Understanding How Men and Women
    Cope Differently With Stress*
Harper (2008)

GRAY, John
What You Can Feel You Can Heal
A Guide for Enriching Relationships
Heart Publishing (1984)

EGGERICHS, Emerson
Love & Respect
The Love She Most Desires, The Respect He Desperately Needs
Thomas Nelson, Inc. (2004)

GOTTMAN, John
and Nan Silver
The Seven Principles for Making Marriage Work
A Practical Guide from the Country's Foremost Relationship Expert
Three Rivers Press (1988)

CITED ARTICLES

BAKER, Amy
**"Helping Children Resist the Pressure To Choose One Parent Over
The Other"**
www.psychologytoday.com (April 8, 2011)

BRENNER, Abigail
**"5 Ways To Create Family Traditions And 5 Reasons Why We
Should"**
www.psychologytoday.com (March 29, 2014)

CASTLEMAN, Michael
**"When She Wants Sex More Than He Does—It's Culturally
Unexpected, But Surprisingly Common"**
www.psychologytoday.com (December 4, 2011)

DIXIT, Jay
**"Sex Ed: The Cheat Sheet—There Are Many Paths To
Unfaithfulness"**
www.psychologytoday.com (February 26, 2010)

KRUK, Edward
**" 'Bird's Nest' Co-parenting Arrangements—When Parents Rotate
In And Out of the Family Home"**
www.psychologytoday.com (July 16, 2013)

KRUK, Edward
**"The Impact of Parental Alienation on Children—Every Child Has A
Fundamental Need For Love and Protection"**
www.psychologytoday.com (April 25, 2013)

LERNER, Harriet
"The Secret To Stop Fighting With Your Partner—Adopt A Distinguished British Houseguest"
www.psychologytoday.com (November 13, 2012)

LERNER, Harriet
"When Fighting Gets Ugly, No Rules Apply But This One—The Number One 'Anger Rule' When Things Go From Zero to One Hundred"
www.psychologytoday.com (March 6, 2014)

NI, Preston
"The #1 Predictor of Divorce (And How To Prevent It)"
www.psychologytoday.com (March 3, 2013)

STOSNY, Steven
"Connection Repair—Strategy vs. Tactics and Maneuvers"
www.psychologytoday.com (January 22, 2014)

TURNDORF, Jamie
"How To Fight Right—How Angry Feelings Can Be Used To Improve Your Relationships"
www.psychologytoday.com (March 6, 2011)

WEINER-DAVIS, Michele
"I Wasn't Looking For An Affair, It Just Happened—Sorry, Infidelity Doesn't Just Happen"
www.psychologytoday.com (May 19, 2008)

INTERNET SOURCES

Ask.com
www.laws.com

Laws.com
www.laws.com

Psychology Today
www.psychologytoday.com

United States Census Bureau
www.census.gov

RESOURCES

Emerson Eggerichs
www.loveandrespect.com

Energy Essentials
Tel: (888) 456-1597
www.energyessentials.isagenix.com

John Gottman
www.gottman.com

John Gray
www.marsvenus.com

Tony O'Donnell
(818) 591–9355
www.radiantgreens.com
email: doctony3@netzero.com

ABOUT THE AUTHOR

D r. Tony O'Donnell is an herbalist–nutritionist, the author of 14 books, and a talk show host. He has a doctorate in psychology, with a Ph.D. in addiction. He can be seen on ABC, NBC, CBS, and FOX, as well as CNN affiliates nationwide. He is the formulator of many leading superfoods, including his amazing green superfood, Radiant Greens.

Dr. Tony holds a 3rd degree black belt in taekwondo and is a martial arts instructor.

Tony's love of people and his willingness to give freely of his time in helping couples fight less and love more is a joy to witness. This is his first relationship book.

Dr. Tony lives in Malibu, California.

Dr. Tony O'Donnell, Ph.D.

WWW.RADIANTGREENS.COM
(818) 575–7558
DOCTONY2014GMAIL.COM